ADVANCE PRAISE FOR *BEYOND THE RINK*

"These three survivors—Kelly, David, and Chris—inspire us not only for what they have done for their communities in the aftermath of the residential school system, but also for showing us how crucial hockey and sports are in bringing Indigenous communities together. Our history and the lessons we've learned are vital, and *Beyond the Rink* does an excellent job of highlighting this."
—Ted Nolan, former NHL Player and Coach, Olympic Coach, and author of *Life in Two Worlds: A Coach's Journey from the Reserve to the NHL and Back*

"This is an unflinching and nuanced look behind the PR veil and a story of loss, triumph, perseverance, tragedy, and memory. It is also a detailed account of the machinery of residential schools and the trauma they inflicted. And it is a revealing look at the power of photographs, which can be used to both illuminate and mislead.

At its heart, *Beyond the Rink* is the story of twelve Indigenous hockey players, who, like their white counterparts, loved the game for the thrill of competition. But they also saw it as an escape from the relentless control and exploitation they faced on a daily basis, even if they were being exploited while playing it. This story is told through the lens of three of the boys, trapped in a world they barely understood, a world that wasn't the least bit interested in understanding them, and in many ways still isn't."
—Gord Miller, TSN

"The authors have spent decades working with the Survivors whose stories they share and centre in this book. *Beyond the Rink* does not simply tell the story of a hockey team; it demonstrates how sport within the context of residential schools was a tool of colonization."
—Karen Froman, University of Winnipeg

"It is difficult to overstate the significance of this book. The scholarship is sound as well as original in context and content, and Survivor testimony is respected and communicated in a theoretically sophisticated way."
—Travis Hay, Mount Royal University

—Michael Bur

Four Little Indians— These boys are members of the Sioux Lookout Black Hawks, who completed a three-game hockey tour here last night, and are shown lacing on their skates prior to a meeting with Shopsy's bantams of the THL. The local team won, 5-1, but failed to damage the spirit of the all-Indian squad, whic returned home last night. Shown above (left to right) ar Jerry Ross, Johnny Yesno (his brother is named Maybe), Kelle Bull and Ernest Wesley. The team covered 2,300 miles on th trip that cost $1,800.

Indian Lads' Hockey Tour Cost $1,800—'Well Worth It'

By BOB FULFORD

From a purely competitive standpoint, Sioux Lookout Black Hawks' 2,300-mile hockey tour could hardly be called a roaring success. But from any other angle it appears well worth the $1,800 it cost.

That, anyway, is the opinion of H. A. Schade, manager of the all-Indian bantam team and one of its principal financiers. After his charges had dropped a 5-1 game to Shopsy's larger hockeyists at the Gardens last night, he declared that, regardless of the two losses (against one win) the Hawks had suffered, he was quite happy.

The trip, which included two games in Ottawa, had been a "wonderful education" for the 10 Ojibways and two Crees from Northern Ontario, he said. "Unless our money runs out—and it won't—we'll have another one next year."

He had an explanation for that loss to the Toronto club, and another for the 8-7 defeat by an Ottawa all-star team Saturday night. He reminded that the Indians had been on their feet since 7 o'clock yesterday morning, attending civic and provincial receptions and several other events, and could hardly be expected to be at their best. The Ottawa game, he said, was so close either team could have won. Just happened the Hawks were one down when the final bell rang.

Shopsy's, a team which, among other things, boasts two players named Tom Kelly, had the advantage in height, weight and speed. tinguished young man besides a promising athlete. A cousin to the two other Wesleys, he is the son of the chief of the Lac Seul band, an Ojibway group.

The happy little fellows from Northern Ontario won the respect and admiration of the crowd and their opponents with a fine display of courage. In the first period they were outclassed but never lost even part of their determination. Though four goals behind in the period's dying moments, they were still playing with everything at their command.

Still, they weren't rough. In fact, they were given no penalties, compared to five issued to the Toronto team.

The player who drew most awed comments from the spectators was 12-year-old Albert Carpenter, smallest member of the team and who, like the other players, re-

Brantford Open Playoff Series Beating Markha

Brantford, April 16. — Brant Burtols, defending champions of OHA Senior "B" series and hol of the Billy Hewitt Cup got a on the right foot here tonigh defeating Markham Milliona 11-2. It's a best-of-seven final se with the second game in Stouff Wednesday night, the home ic the dollar men.

Coach Earl Robinson for Montreal Maroon winger, stated Millionnaires from Markham v played out after their hard se with Kingston Nylons.

The Brantford team was led Wally Hnatiuk who scored t goals and one assist. He chec hard all through the game and an outstanding player, along Billy Simpell the local coach.

Monarchs Defeat

NT Lions Tie

BEYOND THE RINK

Beyond the Rink: Behind the Images of Residential School Hockey

29 28 27 26 25 1 2 3 4 5

University of Manitoba Press
Winnipeg, Manitoba, Canada
Treaty 1 Territory
uofmpress.ca

Cataloguing data available from Library and Archives Canada
Perceptions on Truth and Reconciliation, ISSN 2371-347X ; 6
ISBN 978-177284-106-0 (PAPER)
ISBN 978-177284-108-4 (PDF)
ISBN 978-177284-109-1 (EPUB)
ISBN 978-177284-107-7 (BOUND)

Front cover photograph by Gar Lunney, April 1951, Archives and Special Collections, Western Libraries, Western University. Front section newspaper page detail, *The Globe and Mail*, 17 April 1951, 19. Back cover photograph of a necklace made by Annie Cromarty, courtesy of Alexandra Giancarlo.
Cover Design by Kirk Warren
Interior Design by Karen Armstrong

Printed in Canada

This project was funded by the Social Sciences and Humanities Research Council Insight Grant (435-2016-0713) and the Western Doctoral Fellowship Program.

This book has been published with the help of a grant from the Federation for the Humanities and Social Sciences, through the Awards to Scholarly Publications Program, using funds provided by the Social Sciences and Humanities Research Council of Canada.

The University of Manitoba Press acknowledges the financial support for its publication program provided by the Government of Canada through the Canada Book Fund, the Canada Council for the Arts, the Manitoba Department of Sport, Culture, and Heritage, the Manitoba Arts Council, and the Manitoba Book Publishing Tax Credit.

Funded by the Government of Canada | Canada

BEYOND THE RINK

BEHIND THE IMAGES OF RESIDENTIAL SCHOOL HOCKEY

ALEXANDRA GIANCARLO, JANICE FORSYTH,
AND BRADEN TE HIWI,
WITH THE 1951 SIOUX LOOKOUT BLACK HAWKS

ABBREVIATIONS

CN	Canadian National Railway
DIA	Department of Indian Affairs
MSCC	Missionary Society of the Church of England in Canada
MP	Member of Parliament (Canada)
NAN	Nishnawbe Aski Nation
NCTR	National Centre for Truth and Reconciliation
NFB	National Film Board
NFB SPD	National Film Board Still Photography Division
NHL	National Hockey League
RCMP	Royal Canadian Mounted Police
TRC	Truth and Reconciliation Commission of Canada

CONTENTS

Abbreviations vi

Illustrations ix

Preface: Tea with Kelly (by Janice Forsyth) xv

Introduction: Picturing the Past 1

Much to Hide 4

Learning from the Black Hawks 9

Chapter 1: The Whole Story 13

Why Photographs? 13

Starting at the Beginning 17

Reclaiming Stories, Restor(y)ing Self and Community 24

Chapter 2: The Truth about Photographs 27

Photographing Indigenous People: An Exploitative History 27

Picturing Modern Canada 34

Photographing Indigenous Children at School 38

Chapter 3: Promoting the "Good Work" of Schooling 41

Photographs of Sports 48

Chapter 4: Surviving Pelican Lake 52

A School or a "Workhouse"? 54

Physical Education 60

"A Danger": Health and Illness 62
Order and Discipline 66

Chapter 5: Hockey Will Make Things Better 70
The Unlikely Champions: The Black Hawks, 1948–1951 70
The Symbolism of Indigenous Boys Playing "Canada's Game" 85

Chapter 6: A Means of Escape 89

Chapter 7: Visual Repatriation 104

Epilogue: Picturing the Future
(by Alexandra Giancarlo) 136

Acknowledgements 140

Notes 145

Selected Bibliography 165

Index 173

ILLUSTRATIONS

The players and officials are identified to the best of authors' ability based on Kelly Bull and Chris Cromarty's recollections as well as archival captions.

Figure 1. Chris Cromarty, shown here in 2019, with the newspaper clipping of the Black Hawks that he found in his mother's Bible. Taken by A. Giancarlo and used with permission.__________________ 7

Figure 2. This photo postcard from 190-? demonstrates how the academic "anthropometric" style of photographing Indigenous Peoples sometimes made its way into commercially produced photographs. In turn, these photographs had a wide reach as postcards. Published by D.J.Y. Co. Ltd., Calgary, Alta.; Warwick Bros. and Rutter, Limited, Printers, Toronto. Public domain.____________________ 32

Figure 3. This photo, c. 1901, is from the souvenir photo book *Photographic View Album of Brandon, MB.* Published by W.G. MacFarlane for D.E. Clement, Toronto. Used with permission from the National Gallery of Canada, which holds the original. _____ 37

Figure 4. Looking at this photograph from 194–?, Kelly Bull was prompted to reflect on the labour that had been needed to clear the land to erect the school and all of its buildings. P75-103-S7-125. From the Anglican Church of Canada's Missionary Society of the Church of England in Canada (MSCC) fonds. Reproduced with permission.__56

Figure 5. From Christmas 1946, Chris Cromarty is shown in this photo. He is seated to the right of the tinselled pole with his hand near his face. P7538-1038. From the Anglican Church of Canada's MSCC fonds. Reproduced with permission.____________________ 67

Figure 6. Boys playing outdoors in the winter at Pelican Lake Residential School, c. 1950. Reproduced with permission from

Shingwauk Residential Schools Centre (Algoma University). From an album of photographs that belonged to former Pelican Lake staff member Joyce Clinton. ____ 69

Figure 7. Black Hawks player Ernest Wesley faces off against a player from the Ottawa team during the April 1951 tour. Two ex-NHL players and current members of Parliament who refereed one of the Black Hawks' games, Wilfred "Bucko" McDonald (*right*) and Lionel Conacher (*left*), look on (in white shirts). The man in the dark suit with glasses is Paul Martin Sr. Taken by National Film Board (NFB) photographer Gar Lunney. AFC 451-S5-F14, 56972, 6-5.2-33, 1950–1951. From Archives and Special Collections, Western Libraries, Western University. Used with permission. ____ 75

Figure 8. Black Hawks player Albert Carpenter shakes the hand of an opposing player from the local Ottawa league during the April 1951 tour. Taken by NFB photographer Gar Lunney. AFC 451-S5-F14, 56960, 6-5.2-27, 1950–1951. From Archives and Special Collections, Western Libraries, Western University. Used with permission. ____ 75

Figure 9. Black Hawks Albert Carpenter (*left*) and Ernest Wesley (*right*) pose with former NHL players, and then members of parliament, Wilfred "Bucko" McDonald (*left*) and Lionel Conacher (*right*) during one of the Ottawa games on the April 1951 tour. Taken by NFB photographer Gar Lunney. AFC 451-S5-F14, 56974, 6-5.2-33, 1950–1951. From Archives and Special Collections, Western Libraries, Western University. Used with permission. ____ 76

Figure 10. The Black Hawks in action (shown here in a game in Ottawa, Ontario, during their April 1951 tour). In the centre right, wearing the striped Black Hawks jersey (#12), is Jerry Ross. The other Black Hawk visible on the right side of the image is Eddie Mandamin. Taken by NFB photographer Gar Lunney. AFC 451-S5-F14, 56969, 6-5.2-37, 1950–1951. From Archives and Special Collections, Western Libraries, Western University. Used with permission. ____ 77

Figure 11. Another action shot of the Black Hawks during one of their Ottawa matches on their April 1951 tour. In the centre wearing a striped jersey (#12) is Black Hawks player Jerry Ross. To his right, seen in profile, is likely Black Hawks player Frank Wesley. Further right, with his stick outstretched, is Black Hawk Eddie Mandamin. Taken by NFB photographer Gar Lunney. AFC 451-S5-F14, 56970, 6-5.2-37, 1950–1951. From Archives and Special Collections, Western Libraries, Western University. Used with permission. ________ 78

Figure 12. Cover page of the Black Hawks scrapbook, found in Kelly's collection, for the 1949–1950 season. From the personal collection of Kelly Bull. Used with permission.________ 90

Figure 13. Image of boys playing hockey in the Pelican Lake Indian Residential School's yard in the 1940s. Reproduced with permission from Shingwauk Residential Schools Centre (Algoma University)._92

Figure 14. The Prince Arthur hotel, similar to how it would have looked when Chris Cromarty and the Black Hawks stayed there in February 1951. 975.1.66 Prince Arthur hotel c. "before 1962." Used with permission from the Thunder Bay Museum. ________ 95

Figure 15. This newspaper clipping captures the moment when the Black Hawks met famed hockey player Maurice "The Rocket" Richard in what is now Thunder Bay in July 1951. Chris is third from the right (*front*). David is second from the left. Kelly is directly behind David, with the lower part of his face obscured. This is from an unknown newspaper but would have been either the *Fort William Daily Times-Journal* or the *Port Arthur News Chronicle*, and was found in a scrapbook of Gifford Swartman, former Indian Agent. ________ 95

Figure 16. The swimming pool at the Chateau Laurier from around the time that the Black Hawks stayed at the hotel. 1949. ID Number X-30065. In public domain. Sourced from Ingenium. ________ 99

Figure 17. Kelly Bull, flanked by his teammates and Pelican Lake's Principal Wilson, shakes the hand of the Bishop of Ottawa, Rev. Robert Jefferson. Photograph from the April 1951 tour. *Left to right, in foreground only, with full faces shown*: Frank Wesley, George Carpenter (side profile), Kelly Bull (shaking hand of Bishop), Johnny Yesno, Walter Kakepetum, and Bishop of Ottawa Rev. Robert Jefferson. Taken by NFB photographer Gar Lunney. #2AFC 451-S5-F14,

56955 6-5.2-27, 1950–1951. Archives and Special Collections, Western Libraries, Western University. Used with permission. 99

Figure 18. This newspaper clipping, newspaper unknown, shows the championship-winning hockey team that David Wesley played for upon moving to what is now Thunder Bay, called the Port Arthur North Stars, c. 1953. The clipping was shared with the research team by David Wesley and family. 101

Figure 19. Dating to 1956, this photograph shows a typical hotel room at the Chateau Laurier, similar to what the Black Hawks would have stayed in during their 1951 tour. In public domain. ID Number X-40670. Sourced from Ingenium. 103

Figure 20. An aerial view of the residential school property that shows newly cleared land, the school, and a barn, c. 1927. P75-103, Item Number: S7-130. Used with permission from the Anglican Church of Canada, General Synod Archives Collection MSCC fonds. 103

Figure 21. Portrait of David Wesley taken on the April 1951 tour. Taken by NFB photographer Gar Lunney. Source: AFC 451-S5-F14, 56965, 6-5.2-39, 1950–1951. Archives and Special Collections, Western Libraries, Western University. Used with permission. 106

Figure 22. Portrait of Kelly Bull taken during the April 1951 tour. Taken by NFB photographer Gar Lunney. Source: AFC 451-S5-F14, 56964, 6-5.2-39, 1950–1951. Archives and Special Collections, Western Libraries, Western University. Used with permission. 107

Figure 23. The Black Hawks (1951 or 1952) with personnel; *upper row, left to right*: Indian Agent Gifford Swartman, local businessman and volunteer Oreste Tintinalli, and local businessman and booster Art Schade. Players; *middle row, left to right (standing)*: Lawrence Carpenter, Albert Carpenter, Kelly Bull, Ernest Wesley, Agrippa Beardy. *Front row, left to right (kneeling)*: Frank Wesley, Chris Cromarty, Lawrence Beardy, David Wesley, Walter Kakepetum, Henry Spence, Angus Wesley. AFC 451–3/14.AFC 451-S5-F14, 6-5.2-30, 1950–1951. Reproduced with permission from Western Archives and Special Collections, Western University. 109

Figure 24. Three of the Black Hawks with Jan Eisenhardt, supervisor of physical education and recreation at the DIA, on their April 1951 tour. *Left to right*, Frank Wesley or David Wesley, Johnny Yesno, and Albert Carpenter. Taken by NFB photographer Gar Lunney. AFC 451-S5-F14, 56955, 6-5.2-27, 1950–1951. Reproduced with permission from Archives and Special Collections, Western Libraries, Western University. 110

Figure 25. The Black Hawks' April 1951 tour consisted of visits to institutions of civic importance. This photograph was taken at the Chateau Laurier. The mural, by C.W. Jefferys, was titled "Indians Paying Homage to the Spirit of Chaudiere." *Left to right*: Kelly Bull, David Wesley, unknown (*rear*), George Carpenter, Jerry Ross (*rear*), Ernest Wesley, Johnny Yesno, Walter Kakepetum, and unknown official. Taken by NFB photographer Gar Lunney. Source: AFC 451-S5-F14, 56956, 6-5.2-27, 1950–1951. Archives and Special Collections, Western Libraries, Western University. Used with permission. 112

Figure 26. Newspaper clipping from the *Daily Times-Journal* (Fort William) from 3 July 1951. The float seen in the photograph ("Indian Float") is the one that Chris remembered so vividly. 115

Figure 27. Cow barn at Pelican Lake Indian Residential School, 1948. Copyright expired. No restrictions on use. Online MIKAN no. 4673858. RG10. Volume/box number: 6503. Photographs. Library and Archives Canada. Item no. IND-13-1-94. 117

Figure 28. The bridge from which Kelly and his peers snared fish, 1950. From Archives and Special Collections, Western Libraries, Western University. Used with permission. 120

Figure 29. Kelly identified his brother George in this photograph, c. 1950. Reproduced with permission from Shingwauk Residential Schools Centre (Algoma University). From an album of photographs that belonged to former Pelican Lake staff member Joyce Clinton. 124

Figure 30. The Black Hawks at the National Archives in Ottawa during their April 1951 tour. *Left to right, front row, seated*: George Carpenter, Frank Wesley, Ernest Wesley, possibly Dominion Archivist W. Kaye Lamb, Johnny Yesno, Jerry Ross, and Walter Kakepetum. *Left to right,* *top row, crouching or standing*: Kelly Bull, David Wesley, Henry Spence, Matthew Strang, Eddie Mandamin, and Albert Carpenter. Taken by NFB photographer Gar Lunney. AFC 451-S5-F14, 56953, 6-5.2-27, 1950–1951. From Archives and Special Collections, Western Libraries, Western University. Used with permission. ________________ 126

Figure 31. The Black Hawks watch an unnamed official, possibly MP for Fort William Daniel McIvor, play a musical instrument at Parliament (the House of Commons) during their 1951 tour. Taken by NFB photographer Gar Lunney. AFC 451-S5-F14, 56968, 6-5.2-37, 1950–1951. From Archives and Special Collections, Western Libraries, Western University. Used with permission. ________________ 129

Figure 32. The Black Hawks have dinner at Parliament during their April 1951 tour. The players are, from foreground to background on the left side of the table: George Carpenter, Frank Wesley, Jerry Ross, and Albert Carpenter. On the right side from background to foreground with faces in view: Eddie Mandamin, Walter Kakepetum, David Wesley, and Johnny Yesno. Taken by NFB photographer Gar Lunney. AFC 451-S5-F14, 56957, 6-5.2-27, 1950–1951. From Archives and Special Collections, Western Libraries, Western University. Used with permission. ________________ 130

Figure 33. The Black Hawks pose with Jan Eisenhardt in Ottawa on their April 1951 tour. *Top row, left to right*: Eddie Mandamin, Jerry Ross, Albert Carpenter, Jan Eisenhardt, Frank Wesley, Walter Kakepetum, and Henry Spence. *Bottom row, left to right*: David Wesley, Ernest Wesley, Kelly Bull, Johnny Yesno, Matthew Strang, and George Carpenter. Taken by NFB photographer Gar Lunney. #1AFC 451-S5-F14, 56960 6-5.2-27, 1950–1951. From Archives and Special Collections, Western Libraries, Western University. Used with permission. ________________ 132

Figures 34 a and b: Photograph (front and back) of Chris Cromarty as a young man visiting New York City. Given to authors by Chris Cromarty and used with permission. ________________ 135

PREFACE

TEA WITH KELLY

BY JANICE FORSYTH

Tea and photos. That's how this book began. I was having afternoon tea with Kelly Bull at his house in Timmins, Ontario. The date was Sunday, 10 October 2004. I was attending university in Southern Ontario at the time and had travelled home for the Thanksgiving long weekend. Being home to see family and friends was good for the soul. Kelly and his wife lived about 2.5 kilometres from my parents, so I walked to their house. There was a bright blue sky with hardly any clouds and the temperature hovered just above zero degrees Celsius.

When I entered Kelly's house, he and his wife greeted me warmly as they always did. We sat down at the dining room table and chatted for a while. On the table was a small box, about 8 × 11 inches, that Kelly eventually pulled towards him. He took the cover off to reveal an assortment of black-and-white photographs that were in no obvious order. He asked if he had ever shown me the photographs from his time playing on the Black Hawks hockey team at Sioux Lookout (Pelican Lake) Indian Residential School. I had heard of it, but didn't know much about the large Anglican-run institution in Northwestern Ontario till I started digging into its history shortly after meeting with Kelly. Without giving me a chance to say "no" he continued to pull out the photos, placing them before us on the table. They looked like they were taken by a professional: they had a crisp, clear quality about them, with many being obviously staged. Some depicted bizarre, theatrical-like scenes that felt eerie, ghostly, the same way you sense another presence in the room when your hairs stand on end.

Kelly started by telling me about all the good times he had while playing on that team. He moved from one photo to the next, bringing to life the boys who were pictured in them, reminiscing about who they were as young people with dreams and aspirations, the places they travelled to as a team, the things they saw and experienced away from school, the pranks they pulled, how they helped each other out, and the laughs they shared. He glossed over the adults in the photos, softening their role in his life, as if they weren't important to the story he wanted to share. And in some way, at this precise moment in time, they were irrelevant. He was not focusing on their adult behaviour or how they made him feel, but on his own agency and the agency of his friends, the children who were locked into this complex, lonely space that the camera was trying to hide. Kelly was trying to reclaim the bigger story by focusing on what he could control: his own recollection of what happened at Pelican Lake and what being on the school's hockey team meant to him.

That was the surface. Much more lay beneath what he was trying to say. I sat quietly transfixed, attentive to his emotions, feeling the silences in his story. There were electric undercurrents of unsettledness and confusion, even with his "positive" stories about hockey. This internal turbulence was expressed in the way he kept shifting in his seat when trying to make sense of a troubling thought and in his stillness when he got lost in a particular photo. It resided in the tone of his voice when trying to describe something, in the starts and stops indicating reconsiderations, and in his careful wording, as if he was trying to avoid invisible jagged edges, not just for my benefit, but for his as well. He didn't know yet how to explain parts of his memory, how to integrate being a residential school survivor with being a star athlete on the school's hockey team, where he found solace, support, and pleasure.

The language and theory of reconciling that intricate lived experience eluded him.

That was 2004, when Canadians were still awakening to the existence of Canada's Indian residential school system and the harms that system inflicted upon generations of former students, their families, and their communities. The children who survived their institutionalization were now grown up, trying to rebuild their lives in its aftermath. One year prior, in 2003, Canada implemented the Alternative Dispute Resolution process to provide survivors with a way to address their claims of abuse out of court. A multi-billion-dollar comprehensive claims system, called the Indian Residential Schools Settlement Agreement, would be formally launched several years later, in 2007, but survivors like Kelly were already talking about its promise of a more fulsome response to the abuse they suffered at school and to the system's broader legacy. At the moment, Kelly was unsure if he should sign on to the Alternative Dispute Resolution and try to "put that history behind him"—an understandable strategy that many survivors have probably considered at one point or another—or wait to see what the Settlement Agreement offered.

This was where he turned reflective. He was deeply concerned about which option to choose. He was also concerned about how his experience might be interpreted by people investigating the claims. A lawyer representing the Anglican Church, who was consulting potential claimants in the future Settlement Agreement, had recently visited Kelly at his home, asking about the abuse he had suffered. It was an emotionally draining interview; Kelly had to expose his horrors to someone who showed no real concern for his welfare. Worse, he believed the lawyer might undermine his interests and those of the other survivors whom he was consulting. Kelly explained that as the lawyer was walking out the door he turned around and asked: "Was there anything good at all that came from your time at school?" Without pausing, Kelly answered, "Playing hockey." He went on to describe how through his time playing with the Black Hawks he made lifelong friends, learned how to be part of a team, experienced the value of teamwork, travelled to places he might not otherwise have seen, cherished the joys of winning, and learned from losing. The lawyer took notes, thanked him for his time, and left.

I wrote about this moment in Kelly's life in a 2013 book chapter titled "Bodies of Meaning: Sports and Games at Canadian Residential Schools." Parts of the present book are also excerpted from this 2013 book chapter, with permission. For that chapter I used "Bill" as a pseudonym to protect his privacy. Here is the passage where I describe his thoughts about that moment (and my reaction to his retelling):

> Looking at me across the table, Bill said that maybe he should not have told the lawyer his story about hockey. Could it, he wondered, be used against his claim? Would the lawyers develop a case for sport as a positive effect of the school system and use this argument to deny other applications? I, on the other hand, wondered whether he would suppress these memories, woven as they were into the general narrative structure of abuse that pervades public discussions about residential schools. If these fragments of positive memories were the only good thing that many school survivors had, what might the implications be if the story about how students used sports and games to endure their institutionalization was not shared with other survivors and their families? What impact would this silence have on attempts to bring greater understanding to the legacy of the residential school system in Canada? How important were sports and games and physical activity practices to the broader educational objectives at Indian Affairs? How can research on sports and games at residential schools provide a platform for dealing with this ugly history? At the time, I was simply at a loss for words.[1]

Those photos and the way Kelly talked about them and around them, and my inability to grasp the spaces in between, haunted me for nearly two decades. They also haunted Kelly. We both agreed that playing hockey at Pelican Lake was not merely a "positive" experience, as if, somehow, strapping on the skates and hitting the ice with his teammates made the loneliness, isolation, and fear he felt as a student completely disappear. It certainly didn't stop the physical and sexual abuse he and many other students experienced at that school; Kelly was sexually abused by a male supervisor, a female supervisor, and another student. Nor could we say playing hockey and being a Black Hawks member was a "negative" thing. After all, it sometimes provided him with respite from the things that hurt him at school. Being on that hockey team was something more layered and nuanced. But what? How were we to describe his experience without being trapped by the dichotomy "sport is good" and "school is bad"? That kind of thinking restricted our imaginations. We wondered: How could we explain the complex space of sport in his life and perhaps the lives of other residential school survivors? What mental framework could we assemble to explore their remembrances and, at the same time, place their experiences in the context of cultural genocide, and have the two make sense? We needed a way to ethically address this tension. We needed to build a new way of talking about their experiences, where we neither ignored nor denied their suffering, nor splintered their agency and hope. If Kelly was looking for alternative language to guide his thinking, then I imagined others were too. I know I was.

In the intervening years, we kept returning to that abstract barrier. Along the way, as the number of people working on this project ebbed and flowed, different ideas were shared and tested. We made use of a wide variety of theories and concepts, which also evolved as more scholars, writers, and researchers engaged with the history and legacy of Canada's Indian residential school system and with settler colonialism more broadly.

This book is the culmination of my 2004 conversation with Kelly that began with tea and photos. It also brings to completion nearly twenty years of our research team borrowing, adapting, adjusting, ordering, and reordering the narrative, theories, and concepts that we hope illuminate the struggle Kelly faced when asked a seemingly simple question from a lawyer about whether anything "good" happened to him at school.

Like so many other residential school survivors—mostly men, because they had more opportunities to play sports at school—Kelly still speaks highly of his accomplishments in sports and what he took away from those experiences, especially hockey. But he also understands how sport was used by staff at various levels in the school system to wipe away his attachment to his Anishinaabe (Ojibwe) land base, to his family, and to his culture.

In this book, Kelly pulls his experiences in school and sport apart and puts them back together again. He uses the photographs of the Black Hawks taken by a National Film Board (NFB) photographer on their exhibition tour of Southern Ontario to reconsider the meaning of both sport and schooling in his life. Two of his former teammates, Chris Cromarty and David Wesley, each do the same. This book builds on the graduate work of Fatima Ba'abbad, who also interviewed Chris and Kelly, and Dr. Braden Te Hiwi and the scholarly articles published from his dissertation.[2] Over the course of about four years, Kelly, Chris, and David worked closely with Alexandra Giancarlo, who joined our small team as a postdoctoral associate in 2019 to help us "make sense" of it all. Sam Cronk, Gavin Bennett, and Dr. Evan Habkirk were key parts of our team, contributing design, research, and content-analysis expertise. Dr. Taylor McKee, also an integral part of the research team, joined me, Alexandra, and Braden in our first academic article about the Black Hawks, published in 2021.[3] Some of our research in this book has also appeared in a number of additional articles and book chapters from which we quote freely in this text.[4]

The Black Hawks' stories do not form a neat and tidy narrative about sports somehow being the antidote to dislocation and loss, as many accounts are inclined to do. Rather, they "restory" the existing narrative. They offer deep and nuanced critiques of how sports energized the residential school system by deflecting attention away from what happened behind closed doors and wrapping the children's transformation in a shiny veneer of positivity. This is their story, now more than seventy-four years after being Black Hawks.

INTRODUCTION

PICTURING THE PAST

In May 2021, the news of the discovery of more than two hundred suspected unmarked graves at Kamloops Residential School in British Columbia sent convulsions across Canadian society. The public seemed to be waking up to the reality that describing residential schools as tools of genocide was not a metaphor. Many residential school survivors and intergenerational survivors found themselves tossed into the deep waters of grief, unspeakable sadness, and anger. Upon hearing the first news reports, Kelly longed for more detail. He asked Alexandra: Had this been some kind of massacre? At first, he could not remember anyone going missing at Pelican Lake Residential School, but on reflection, one student with whom he frequently spent time in the infirmary *had* seemed to vanish overnight. Commenting on the powerlessness the students lived with, Kelly later remarked that "for all we knew, he could have been six feet underground." Chris recalled that he had heard about, and witnessed, students running away from the school by hopping on a train. He had always assumed they had made it home, but now wondered otherwise. He reported a deep sadness, a sense of helplessness, and feelings of guilt that he had made it out of the school when others had not. He felt humble, and grateful, to have survived.

The entire residential school system was predicated on the assumption that Indigenous Peoples would not survive—in a cultural, if not literal, sense. Though the system of over one hundred schools was made up of institutions that differed by geography, religious denomination, and size, all were united in the goals of interrupting the transmission of Indigenous cultural knowledge and practices across generations. They also all aimed to prepare Indigenous children for their roles as assimilated Canadian citizens. During the same decade as the Black Hawks' famous tour, continuous and total isolation ("ideally twenty-four hours a day and twelve months of the year") from Indigenous culture and home communities was recommended to ensure the schools' success.[1] These cultural prohibitions were harshly, even violently, enforced, such as when the Pelican Lake principal slugged Chris from behind after he was caught speaking a few words of Ojibwemowin (the Ojibwe language) to a family picking up their child from school.

Meanwhile, the extensive manual labour that students had to undertake, such as that described by the Black Hawks, meant that their education suffered greatly. The labour both reduced their educational opportunities while at school and had the consequence of limiting their post-school career options to lower-paying fields. As a result, many survivors found that the types of paths increasingly open to Euro-Canadian graduates of the same period, such as attending university, were closed to them. Chris and Kelly had not even been permitted to choose whether they wanted to attend a collegiate high school instead of the technical-vocational institution to which they were sent, not realizing until much later that many of their high school credits were not valid prerequisites for the university level.

In an atmosphere in which they had so little control and so few opportunities for genuine achievement, hockey was a lifeline. From the perspective of policy makers at the Department of Indian Affairs (DIA) headquarters, competitive sports such as hockey contributed to the Branch's goals of assimilation by bringing Indigenous boys into contact with white society, presumably so that the former would learn from the latter. Traditional recreational and physical culture activities would not do and needed replacing with something "wholesome." "Modern" sports, like hockey and football, were thought to teach Indigenous students the traits they would need for modern society, and which were considered to be lacking in their communities of origin and in their traditional physical activities: respectability, obedience, and team spirit. At the school administrative level, by the 1950s, hockey was favoured as it seemed to decrease student runaways and increase student compliance with the rules that governed life at the institution. Since students understood that participating in hockey was a privilege that not all students had access to, it also gave the staff at Pelican Lake leverage over their pupils. In short, hockey was both a tool of discipline (from the perspective of the administration) and a tool of temporary liberation (from the perspective of the Black Hawks).

Much evidence from residential schools across history testifies to their "two-sided" nature: one constructed for visitors, the media, and the public, and the other for the students who experienced daily life at these institutions. A short-lived employee of the Round Lake Indian School in Saskatchewan—who we would now call a "whistleblower"—was fired after reporting the shocking conditions to church headquarters. She explained that "to almost everything at Round Lake, there is the two sides, the side that goes in the report and that inspectors see, and the side that exists from day to day in the actual working out."[2] Among other horrors, she reported that the children received about three tablespoons of porridge for breakfast and that the boys had to go to the bathroom in a pail because the water closets (toilets) had been broken for months.[3]

Public image was paramount. For example, an inspector evaluating the Birtle Residential School in Manitoba expressed disapproval at the raggedness of the children's clothing, but assured headquarters that the children do have proper clothes "for Sundays and when the children go down town—in other words, when out where they can be seen, they are well dressed."[4] By 1949, when Arthur Bear Chief attended Old Sun Residential School in southern Alberta, the public-facing performance had gained a new sophistication. While a film crew was on site, the younger boys were pulled into a fictional bedtime routine that included cookies and a glass of milk before bed. As he summed up, "everything was staged."[5]

This exploration with the Black Hawks offers a rare glimpse behind the veil that shielded the public from the truth of the student experience at these institutions. Returning these historic photographs into the hands of the players facilitates the opportunity to tell their truths, both the consequences of unfulfilled potential and the stories of survival, of coping with the demons from the past, and having the courage to reclaim their stories for themselves and their communities today.

The official images of the 1951 tour conveyed a tidy narrative of assimilation. To paraphrase photographer Gar Lunney's words, it was a story told visually. The Black Hawks respond to and challenge this colonial gaze. They "restory" the visual tale told by the NFB and the DIA, creating a new narrative that "transcends the stories and power structures" dictated by the photos' origin and purpose.[6] Disrupting this narrative "ensures personal and cultural survival, as individuals and communities root themselves in their own understandings of the past and, as a result, gain a sense of agency and empowerment in the present and future."[7] Speaking back to these photographs, as the Black Hawks have done, creates new presences in public memory and challenges the "official" historical narrative. The Black Hawks insist on telling "our histories"[8]—histories that foreground the intimate, and difficult, stories of their people. When asked about whether the research team should hold back sensitive details about his experiences at Pelican Lake, Chris insisted that everything be told "because it really happened."

Much to Hide

> What do we read in pictures?
>
> Most of us, very little. Perhaps we see a house, a man, an animal, a flower. We see so little, when in every picture there is a whole story, the background, the foreground, the main subject.
>
> Will you read the pictures in this little book? At first glance they are just pictures of boys and girls. Perhaps you are particularly interested because some of them are your boys and girls, perhaps you do not even know any of them. Whether

> you know them or not, they all have their story to tell you and it is well worth the reading.
>
> *Read these pictures slowly and carefully—get the story from every face, then put the stories together and you will have one of the truly great stories of the Missionary Educational Enterprise of the Church and Government in Canada.*[9]

Photographs have much to tell us—and much to hide. The above passage, an introduction to a 1946–47 yearbook for Brandon Indian Residential School in Manitoba, hints at what readers can expect to learn from the photographs inside. The reader should be able to know "their story"—the experiences of the boys and girls, both smiling and unsmiling, photographed by grade in neat rows throughout the slim volume. Taken together, these photographs are supposed to form a cohesive account: "one of the truly great stories" of the residential school system.

We can also read alternative and conflicting messages in these images. Did the students agree that their yearbook images told "one of the truly great stories" of the Indian residential school system? Doubtful. If this was a great story, it was a one-sided narrative, told without the voices of the students.

Residential school photographs do have stories to tell that are "well worth the reading," but they are much different stories than most school administrators would have envisioned. Take, for example, a well-worn photograph in a newspaper clipping of the Black Hawks. It appeared in the *Port Arthur News-Chronicle*'s Saturday, 17 February 1951, edition, with the title "All-Indian Team Here." Pictured are twelve pre-teen boys, all smiling, and three adult men, who seem to be pleased with the attention their team is getting. In the description that goes along with the photograph, the men are identified, along with their official connection to the team and standing in local society. Readers learn a little bit about who they are and their role in providing the boys with this opportunity. The boys, on the other hand, remain nameless. The only relevant detail provided is that they are from the Anglican Indian Residential School near Sioux Lookout.

Aside from the fact that the boys are Indigenous, it could be any unremarkable amateur hockey team photo from that era. But the creases and rips from the many viewings suggest this photograph and news article is something special. For Chris Cromarty, who is in the front row, this clipping—the piece of worn newspaper with the hockey photograph and part of its accompanying story—is something of an anchor, a physical link to a past now more than seventy years distant that still feels very current to him. As one of the few items that Chris possesses that had belonged to his mother, it is also symbolic of her memory and of their strong emotional connection, which remains intact. The photograph in the clipping is even more important because it is one of the few pictures Chris has of himself on the team. Chris was not selected for the team that travelled to Ottawa and Toronto in April of 1951, so his first-hand recollections throughout this book centre on hockey experiences at Pelican Lake itself and from participating in games and tournaments throughout northern Ontario.

Chris discovered the newspaper clipping in his late mother's Bible (Figure 1). His brother, who had been institutionalized at the Fort William (present-day Thunder Bay) Sanatorium after contracting tuberculosis, sent it to her. While Chris was at Pelican Lake during the school year, he was unable to communicate with his parents, as they could not read English and he could not write in Cree syllabics. His mother would not have been able to understand what was written in the newspaper article, nor would she have understood the context of the photograph. She was not familiar with the sport of hockey and Chris did not have any regular contact with home while at school. The image itself, then, would have had special meaning as both the only news of her son and the only part of the clipping that was easily understandable: Chris was dressed in neat clothing, smiling. Even if the deeper meanings around hockey would not have been entirely clear to her, it bore news of her son who was alive and seemed to be well looked after by the adults in the image. (Kelly elaborated on Chris's points here and explained that, in his recollection, students did write home—in fact, they were compelled to at semi-regular intervals. They wrote letters

Figure 1. Chris Cromarty, shown here in 2019, with the newspaper clipping of the Black Hawks that he found in his mother's Bible. Taken by A. Giancarlo and used with permission.

in English that followed a script on the blackboard that suggested, in Kelly's words, that "things were just peachy.")

But there is another layer of meaning here. The circulation of this clipping from his brother to his mother—and, eventually, back to Chris himself—was the only tenuous connection between the family members separated by the forces of the Canadian government's colonial policies set in motion in the 1800s: his mother in remote Northern Ontario, his older brother in the Fort William Sanatorium, and he at residential school. In fact, Chris did not know his older brother very well. His brother "never was well enough to stay at home from the time he left residential school. He spent all his time at the sanatorium" and died in his early twenties. It was not until the 1990s that Chris learned that his brother and father, who also died in the sanatorium, had been buried in an unmarked plot in a Thunder Bay cemetery.

The photograph that appeared in the newspaper clipping that circulated within his family symbolized the complicatedness, as well as the simplicity, of Chris's family's story. Outside forces that tore his family apart created complexities that affect them to this day. At the same time, his story is filled with easy-to-understand messages of love and hope and continuance. His family history is not uncommon. It is mirrored in the histories of countless Indigenous families and communities who strained under the weight of colonialism and who still found ways to build better lives and communities despite all they went through. That is one of the other "great stories" that went untold for decades about the residential school system: the reclamation and regeneration of their identities and lives as Indigenous Peoples.

Above, Principal Strapp, the likely author of the introduction to the 1946–47 yearbook for the Brandon Indian Residential School wrote that "in every picture there is a whole story." Perhaps he would have liked his audience—most likely the DIA, members of the United Church of Canada, potential donors, and parents of the children attending the school—to believe that the yearbook images confirmed the "whole story" of life at the residential school. As residential school survivors, their families, communities, and researchers continue to unpack residential school evidence, including the use of photographs in the school system, we will approach something closer to the "whole story" of that system and its effects on individuals, families, and society.

Learning from the Black Hawks

The following section, Chapter 1: The Whole Story, has us "going in deeper"—to use Kelly's words—to examine the historical events that propelled colonization. From here, we dive into why and how photographs are at the heart of the Black Hawks' retelling of their lives on the hockey team. Chapter 2: The Truth about Photographs helps the reader to understand the photos taken of the Black Hawks on their tour within the longer history of colonial photography of Indigenous and other colonized peoples. What is important here is the effect of this imagery on Western viewers who came to see this type of photography as a true representation of Indigenous lives as, predominantly, uncivilized and in need of the "uplifting" influence of Christianity—typified by the residential school system. In Chapter 3: Promoting the "Good Work" of Schooling, we turn to the policy context that led to a brief flurry of interest and resources being dedicated to competitive team sports at residential schools in the period following the Second World War. We examine how images of students playing sports conveyed distinct messages to the Canadian public that offered visual validation of the DIA's policy goals, as well as what these photos hid. Chapter 4: Surviving Pelican Lake examines the difficult history of the institution and the boys' lives within it. We see how consistent underfunding and apathy drove poor student health, abuse, and a reliance on student labour. Importantly, we hear first-hand from the Black Hawks, speaking through the prism of photographs, about how they coped with life at what Kelly has called "a mausoleum." Chapter 5: Hockey Will Make Things Better delves into the 1951 tour in earnest, with special consideration of how the Black Hawks were portrayed in the press given the symbolism of Indigenous boys excelling in "Canada's game." The Black Hawks' restorying is front and centre in Chapter 6: A Means of Escape, where the reader learns what hockey meant to David, Chris, and Kelly as they struggled to endure the grim conditions of life at Pelican Lake Residential School. Chapter 7: Visual Repatriation grounds the

Black Hawks' story in the currents of global Indigenous movements to reclaim and restory colonial visual archives. Through their retellings of the tour and their lives as hockey players, the Black Hawks reshape an assimilation story into a story of survival, resilience, and cultural pride.[10]

First, we begin with a brief biography of each of the players. Chris, Kelly, and David have varying levels of experience with telling their stories publicly, and varying levels of participation in this project due to Covid-19-related travel restrictions, health issues that the elderly men experienced, and challenges in accessing rural and remote residences. One other player is still living and was not interested in participating, having already told his story to his community and others who are important to him.

Chris Cromarty was born in Kitchenuhmaykoosib Inninuwug (formerly Big Trout Lake) in 1937 and grew up speaking Anisininew (Anishininimowin, formerly known as Oji-Cree). He also learned Ojibwe (Ojibwemowin) when his family moved off-reserve in 1944 to the mining town of Pickle Crow. He attended Pelican Lake Indian Residential School from 1945 to 1952 and Shingwauk Indian Residential School from 1952 to 1956. Chris spent a lifetime serving his people. He was one of the founders of the Nishnawbe Aski Nation (NAN) in 1973, then known as Grand Council Treaty #9, a political organization that represents the interests of forty-nine First Nations in Northern Ontario.[11] Chris served, as well, as its first Deputy Grand Vice Chief. In the late 1990s, he was the first board chair of the Sioux Lookout Meno Ya Win Health Centre, bringing a team of Indigenous and non-Indigenous professionals together to envision and build a joint health centre in the region. In 2007, Meno Ya Win honoured Chris with its inaugural leadership award, named after him. He also participated in the public testimony portion of the Truth and Reconciliation Commission. Chris, who passed away in June 2022, always spoke proudly and fondly of his community service and of the foster children that he and his wife, Annie, raised. His absence is keenly felt across all the communities he touched, including our research team—and especially by Alexandra, with whom he formed a deeper friendship.

Kelly Bull is Ojibwe from Obishikokaang (Lac Seul First Nation), is a fluent Ojibwemowin speaker, and is a member of the Bear Clan. He attended Pelican Lake Indian Residential School for eight years and Shingwauk Indian Residential School for six years. After graduation, he became a strong advocate for sports and recreation in Indigenous communities and worked for NAN as their Recreation Director. Highlights from his career in promoting Indigenous recreation were forming the Ontario Aboriginal Sports Circle in the 1970s and being part of the larger council that conceived the North American Indigenous Games, which continues to be the premier sporting event for Indigenous Peoples in North America. Kelly and his wife, Greta, who passed away in 2017, have two children and one granddaughter.

David Wesley hails from Fort Albany First Nation. He attended Pelican Lake Indian Residential School and Shingwauk Indian Residential School until Grade 8 in 1953. He was then sent to Fort William-Port Arthur (now Thunder Bay) by the DIA to play hockey. Considered by the press and his teammates to be one of the star players on the Black Hawks, David went on to play for the Port Arthur North Stars and then the Port Arthur Bearcats, with whom he was Rookie of the Year. A severe head injury put an end to his goal of becoming a professional hockey player. In later decades, he was closely involved in building a hockey arena in Cochenour, Ontario, near where he worked as the area mine's Native Employment Coordinator. David married Elga Leveque, with whom he had six children, and who passed away in 2007. In later years David married Elise, and they enjoyed many years of blended family life together, with dozens of grandchildren and great-grandchildren, before her passing in 2021.

CHAPTER 1

THE WHOLE STORY

Why Photographs?

Photographs obviously sit at the heart of this retelling, serving as both the inspiration for embarking on this project and as the objects through which the survivors reflected on the past and the future. The set of about a dozen photographs that were the inspiration for this project—the collection that Kelly Bull pulled from his box when Janice visited for tea in 2004—were taken in April 1951 by Gar Lunney, one of the leading photojournalists in the NFB's Still Photography Division ("the Division").

The research team's goal was to support the players to use the photo collection of the Black Hawks to "make sense of [the] past . . . and make it fulfil the needs of the present."[1] Research projects have shown that Indigenous engagement with historical photographs can reveal lost ancestors, validate previously hidden stories and experiences, and help explain the meaning of the past in present-day lives.[2] The process used to create new stories was to bring our set of residential school photographs, most of which were related to the 1951 hockey tour, to spark memories and conversations with the survivors.

In this way, the returning of photos to survivors was a process of visual repatriation, the term for the return of historical images from museum or private collections to source communities for re-interpretation.[3]

Other research studies have been successful in using photos to generate new stories with Indigenous communities. For instance, photos have helped to produce new knowledge of community and individual histories lost to the powerful forces affecting First Nations in early twentieth century Canada, such as the case of repatriating anthropological portraits taken of members of the Kainai Nation as white settlement, industrialization, and residential schooling abruptly shifted their traditional ways.[4] Although many researchers use photos from museums, archives, and newspapers, Anishinaabe scholar Pedri-Spade used photos from the community members themselves.[5] She learned that engaging with these images sparked cultural teachings that had been suppressed due to the effects of residential schools on spirituality and language.

The former Black Hawks use the photos to offer reflections and wisdom on cultural pride, courage, and perseverance against overwhelming odds. Similarly, Indigenous Australians' engagement with photos from the colonial period had a restorative or healing value, even though the photographs were produced under extremely difficult circumstances.[6] When used alongside Indigenous stories, photographs can be part of a technology of Indigenous memory that sheds light on "secret and silent histories" and a past distorted by colonialism.[7]

Though the Division's repository was primarily accessed by federal Canadian agencies, the private sector and individuals could also access it. Photographs, such as those of the Black Hawks, had worldwide reach through distribution by the Canadian Department of Foreign Affairs. Others are archived and digitally accessible through archives such as the Shingwauk Residential Schools Centre. The Anglican Church has the image included here as Figure 17 in its digital archives. The images of the tour also circulated through social and familial networks, such as within the family of Gifford Swartman, then Indian Agent of the district home to Pelican Lake Indian Residential School.

Created by an Act of Parliament in 1939, the NFB made extensive use of iconic imagery to shape ideas about the nation, such as prairie grain elevators and the vast Northern landscape, famous Canadian figures, and ordinary people doing ordinary things.[8] Indeed, the NFB's founder, John Grierson, was acutely aware of the potential of documentary to shape public opinion. Grierson promoted documentary film and photography "as a tool to serve the state."[9] The NFB was thus as much a part of the government machinery as was the DIA, serving as a public relations tool of the federal government.[10]

The Division used photography as its medium to help the NFB fulfill its mandate. From 1941 to 1971, the Division took more than 25,000 photographs that were disseminated widely through newspapers, magazines, television, film, books, and exhibitions, so that most if not all Canadians during this time learned something about Canada through the Division's work. In the early 1950s, the NFB had a firm focus on national identity, using photography to promote an uplifting, invigorating, and celebratory vision of the nation. These were not the images of Canada as the people saw it, struggling as they were with the ravages of the Second World War and the Cold War—and, for Indigenous Peoples, the continuous shocks of settler colonialism. This was "Canada" through the government's eyes—an idealized version that was meant to show citizens who they should be and how they should act. The overall picture the Division created was of a young, vibrant, culturally diverse, resource-rich country, full of healthy, happy, hard-working people.

As he saw it, Lunney, who photographed the Black Hawks, believed the photographers' job at the NFB was "to show Canada to Canadians."[11] Indeed, NFB staff took their mission—to connect geographically and culturally distinct Canadians to one another and to the ideals of Canadian nationhood—very seriously. The official images of the Black Hawks' tour that Lunney took suggested the government was playing an important, positive role in Indigenous people's lives by exposing their children to all of the "good" things modern, urban Canada could provide: education, jobs, health, friends, happiness, and a comfortable lifestyle. Lunney commented that during this era, he and his colleagues at the NFB desired to portray the nation, and their aspirations for it, as "one big happy family."[12] The fact that the NFB still exists today speaks to the ongoing importance the federal government still attaches to imagery for nation-building purposes.

On 11 April 1951, the Black Hawks set out from Sioux Lookout by train to undertake the long journey to Southern Ontario. The train took the team along the transcontinental railway line and, since its scheduled stop in Sioux Lookout was in the middle of the night, the boys and their chaperones had prepared by spending the previous night in a sleeper car ready for pickup when the train reached their station. Accompanying the players were the school principal (Reverend Scott Wilson), the mayor of Sioux Lookout and team president (William Fuller), the Indian Agent and team secretary-treasurer (Gifford Swartman), regular coach Bruce McCully, a former professional player serving as tour coach (Johnny McDonald), and a local entrepreneur who was team manager (Arthur Schade). They arrived in Ottawa at Union Station in the early morning of 12 April. They were received by Ottawa's mayor, Grenville W. Goodwin, and had lunch in the House of Commons. They played two games while in Ottawa and then one in Toronto, where they had the unforgettable experience of playing at the Maple Leaf Gardens.

Lunney, from the NFB, was part of the team's news coverage. His photographs of the Black Hawks were at times mundane, as with some of the team photos, and at other times singularly extraordinary, especially when the boys were meeting dignitaries or being taught a history lesson. Media reports of the Black Hawks provided a public relations opportunity to spread positive messaging about residential schools, validating the system's existence.[13]

Hockey provided the central visual cues that gave the 1951 tour symbolic force. Without hockey to pull everything together, the tour would have been another unremarkable educational expedition by the DIA, probably heavily criticized for its extravagance. Hockey, and the symbolism it provided, especially when represented in "civilized" contexts like art, education, politics, and health, was the key to the tour's success. The game's links to Euro-Canadian culture—and the resulting implications of images of Indigenous children playing the game so well—are abundant. The images of the Black Hawks enjoying Canada's favourite national pastime is additional evidence that the photographs were meant to align with the "governmental vision of a cohesive Canada."[14] In the eyes of sports reporters and minor league sports representatives, "public concern about the nation's children (particularly the nation's boys) and their physical, mental, and moral development" was quieted by youth sport, as it promoted "proper" masculine norms.[15]

The Black Hawks as hockey players would have had specific cultural meaning for Canadian viewers in the early 1950s, when the sport became an important part of everyday life for many Canadians. Hockey's power as a unifying symbol grew during the 1950s, when *Hockey Night in Canada* became one of the most popular radio shows of the time and an increasing number of households boasted home television sets. After the Second World War, church groups, businesses, and civic organizations like Lions Clubs formed a broad foundation of support for organized hockey for the nation's boys and young men.

The Black Hawks did not know that they were a small but important part of this nation-building program. To them, they were simply going on the trip of a lifetime to play a game they loved. While on tour, they met with people of high status in Canadian culture, such as the Governor General, and did so in places of national importance, such as Parliament Hill and the National Archives.[16] The Black Hawks' coach and workshop teacher, Bruce McCully, was so thrilled with the educational value of the tour, he commented that "these three days in Ottawa will be worth three years' schooling for the boys."[17]

Starting at the Beginning

Times *are* different now than they were nearly twenty years ago when Janice had tea with Kelly. The world is not only ready for a story like this, but it needs stories like these, because as residential schools are again in the headlines, so too are disturbing narratives that seek to downplay, or deny altogether, the system's worst effects. It is time to tell this story because it offers a more thorough way of looking at residential school experiences and understanding how totalizing these institutions were. Kelly reflected, "I think the thing that upsets me most is the denial. . . . Why do we have to go through this to prove that it did happen? And who is on the other side? Are they listening?"

The survivors were adamant that this book tell "the whole story" about being a Black Hawk. Quite quickly, the research team realized that telling the whole story went beyond telling a hockey story. For Chris, the whole story largely meant the broader conditions of life at the school. For Kelly, the whole story meant starting at the beginning: "You started out to educate the public about Native people and the hard times they've come through. It's the *reasons* that we should be telling. Why were there residential schools in the first place? When I listen to some of those critics on the television and radio, they have no idea."

Scholars have pointed out that while the residential school system had a beginning and end, its legacy is more difficult to identify "because the creators of the system wanted their effects to complement larger, parallel processes of settler colonization."[18]

One of the most significant actions that accelerated the colonization of the Americas was the Doctrine of Discovery, technically a series of papal bulls or charters issued by the Pope, that gave certain rights to Portugal and Spain "on the basis of discovery and conquest" beginning in the 1400s.[19] The two interrelated principles underlying the European claims to wide swaths of the world were relatively straightforward. First, Europeans believed that their Christian God had given them the authority to colonize the parts of the world that they "discovered," as long as the people native to these lands were converted to Christianity. Second, they considered themselves to be the bearers of "civilization." In other words, "it was contended that people were being colonized for their own benefit, either in this world or the next."[20] The fact that Christianity underpinned colonization made sense to Kelly, who experienced the effects of these policies so intimately. Kelly had noted the hypocrisy of the behaviour of the Christian figures in charge of Pelican Lake:

> Christianity was thrown, shoved in our face so forcefully. I got to the point where [I began to think] "Those are some pretty nice words the Minister is saying" until one day . . . we had done all our chores and we were in the church chapel. And I think the sermon that the Minister was preaching was "Love thy neighbor as thyself" and it made a lot of sense to me. I said, "Well, maybe that's where I picked up being nice

> to people," until about an hour or so later [when] we were out in the playground . . . the principal happened to be walking around amongst kids playing. And he heard two boys conversing with each other in Indian and you should have seen him. Boy, did he give it to them. And I stood there, and I watched, and I said, "Holy smokes. What's going on here? Here's a guy that just finished telling us to love thy neighbor as thyself and he's pounding the hell out of two defenceless boys." . . . I think from that point on I was starting to have doubts in the message coming down from their lips.

Another idea closely complemented the Doctrine of Discovery: *terra nullius* (land belonging to no one). Colonists argued that Indigenous Peoples did not have ownership of the lands that they inhabited. This definition of "ownership" originated from European property regimes and dictated that only through agriculture, not occupation, could lands be technically "owned." In fact, by using this notion the British government "claimed" the entire Australian continent.[21] In the late nineteenth and early twentieth centuries, settler occupation required increasing amounts of land, said to be empty and freely available, which in turn required displacement of Indigenous Peoples.[22]

It should be emphasized, therefore, that the residential school system "was but one aspect of a much larger settler colonial project, which used coercive instruments, including starvation, forced removal, and the concentration of peoples onto small and isolated reserves, often away from fertile lands, which the government then opened up to European settlement."[23] An overriding concern evident in the government's rationale for its policies towards Indigenous Peoples was the reduction of its financial obligations to them,[24] as well as obtaining formerly Indigenous-held lands to be sold for profit.[25] Kelly understood these financial motives: "Why do you suppose they want to get rid of the Indian people? Because we were a drain [on] the pocketbooks of the government. And I think they knew that there was a lot more to what the treaties addressed. There was wealth under the ground. *Oil.* Minerals. Damming of the rivers for power. And so forth."

Researchers have argued that, beginning in the late 1800s, "Indigenous child-rescue" was a key element of state formation for settler colonies.[26] They have further argued that child removal was not an afterthought but a *central part* of colonial policy: a "priority through which they sought to manage colonial subjects and shape and maintain the social order."[27] Before 1883, residential schools existed as individual church-run educational facilities that received operating grants from the federal government. But in that year, the federal government announced their plans to open and fund three schools on the prairies.[28]

In the United States and Canada, the removal of Indigenous children with the goal of "redeeming" them through labour and Christianity was common thinking. Indigenous communities, and especially Indigenous mothers, were thought to be a uniquely detrimental influence.[29] By casting Indigenous parents as backward, the state and churches justified "rescuing" Indigenous children from their own families and communities and claimed that these actions would benefit the children by preparing them for modern society.[30] Kelly bristled at the paternalistic assumptions that guided this policy, asking, "What gives them the right to assume?"

The Indian Act of 1876 limited many of the political rights of Indigenous Peoples within the new country of Canada and cemented the government's paternalistic approach to Indigenous Peoples, whom John A. Macdonald had characterized as child-like dependants instead of treaty partners.[31] The provisions of the Indian Act had direct and dramatic consequences in the legal, cultural, spiritual, and educational lives of Indigenous Peoples; it had been designed as "a complete code for the management of Indian Affairs."[32]

The Act and its many amendments established the chief-and-council system, enacted gendered definitions dictating who could hold Indian status, and severely restricted or banned Indigenous spiritual ceremonies such as the potlatch and the Sundance.[33] It also made clear that the main thrust of the Canadian government's relationship with Indigenous Peoples was assimilation. Indigenous men could become enfranchised as full citizens, thus giving up their Indian status, though the reverse could not occur—meaning that there was no legal process by which an enfranchised person or his descendants could again become an "Indian."[34]

Kelly rightfully identifies the Indian Act as one of the most substantial assaults on Indigenous life and rights that has occurred since settlers arrived in what is now Canada. Central to the story of the Black Hawks, the Indian Act and subsequent amendments required Indigenous children to attend residential, boarding, or day schools, first until the age of sixteen (1894 amendment) and later between the ages of seven and fifteen (1920 amendment).[35]

Consequently, while hockey provided the binding symbols that gave the Black Hawks 1951 tour meaning, the broader story, from the Black Hawks' perspective, links their residential school experiences to the erasure of Indigenous histories and identities in Canada all the way back to the Doctrine of Discovery. Kelly understood that the Doctrine of Discovery set in motion a series of historical events that were catastrophic for his ancestors' way of life because they set the stage for the treaties and the taking of Indigenous lands. The Doctrine of Discovery was responsible for the eventual erasure of all things Indigenous, epitomized by the residential school system that robbed him of his culture, community, and family life. In some of his notes reflecting on this project that he later shared with the research team, Kelly wrote, "assimilation means the annihilation of Indian nations." He encouraged the research team to take a longer view to understand that the Black Hawks' story started much, much earlier. As these discussions progressed, he remarked, "I like what I'm hearing. I see more [in this project] than what I had envisioned before. I was starting to question you guys: is it just hockey we are talking about here? You guys are going in deeper. You want to know the reasons why. Who are the perpetrators and why was this done?"

The tour, as imagined through the lens of NFB photographer Lunney, was a story. We know this, in part, from Lunney's own words in interviews with former NFB employees archived at the National Gallery of Canada. When asked how one tells a story in pictures, Lunney replied: "It's simple. You say to yourself, 'what is this all about? What do you want me to do with this?' I'm not going to write a story. I have to do it *visually.*"[36] In his hands, Lunney's camera told the story of a successful transformation of identity, from Indigenous to "Canadian." This narrative captured how the DIA, in its partnership with the NFB, used photographs of Indigenous Peoples to, in one scholar's words, "illustrate a unifying transformation"[37] that was underway: "from 'primitive' to 'civilized.'"[38]

In contrast, Kelly, Chris, and David's stories insist on the humanity that colonialism tried to strip away. If the tour and its photos contributed to public erasure of Indigenous histories and cultures, through the Black Hawks' stories this book aims to counter that erasure. The Black Hawks' stories include what came before—the lives that they had left behind when they were forced to attend school—and what came after. However, this book is not a detailed biography, as some books are, but rather captures how they feel and think about their experiences more than seventy years later. While paying attention to the nuances of the stories and experiences they were recounting, the survivors each used the photos to tell a story both personal and educational. These stories are deeply personal for Kelly, Chris, and David. However, they are also part of the wider arc of residential school narratives, Indigenous history, and Canadian history. As the three survivors "picture the past" by using images in telling the Black Hawks story, they also assert a place for themselves in the story of our nation.

As such, this book tells three distinct but interrelated stories about Kelly, Chris, and David—how they each remember and speak about their time at school and being on the team. Engaging with the images brought the players back to a time long before the lawyers and the litigation, public testimonies, and settlements. Looking back at the photos after everything they have been through in the intervening years, there is much that these photos reveal and much that they hide. The survivors' stories are fragmented and moving in their own way, especially in the silences that remain. Taken together, they offer a complex story about the Indian Residential School System, the role of sports and physical activities in the system, their lasting effects, and how Canadians can respond responsibly today. Their words also open a door to understanding throughlines from the past to the present, from exploitation that began with the Doctrine of Discovery, saw its later expressions in the Indian Act and residential schools, and endures to the present through unclean water on reserves and broken promises from the federal government.

Kelly remains skeptical about the sincerity of the government's apology for the harms of the residential school system. He recalled watching the pomp and circumstance of the 2008 apology on TV. In speaking about that day with Alexandra, he remarked in a dismayed tone, "There were crimes that were committed." His tone suggested disbelief that this was all the official action that would be taken.

Kelly, Chris, and David speak about their experiences in ways that do not indicate a belief in "closure." Today, Kelly wonders how one defines "closure" and if that definition might be based on a Western worldview, not an "Indian" one. Still, he says, "I want to tell the world that this is what happened." The words of a scholar who worked with Minnesota Ojibwe people on a photography-based community history project are insightful. He explained: "The overall goal in studying these photographs is not to answer all the questions and, in doing so, provide closure, but [instead] to provide an opening."[39]

This project is a co-creation, a research model that is becoming more common in projects with Indigenous people and communities. This model is based on "mutual learning, sharing, and knowledge production," three key elements of ethical research involving Indigenous Peoples.[40] The Black Hawks "are not just informants but also experts and co-narrators in the research," in the words of a team of Indigenous community members and researchers in Australia describing their own arrangement.[41] While our approach is collaborative, we know that a complete equalization of power relations is not possible. Collaborative visual methods can, however, lead to new and potentially liberating outcomes.

We are fortunate to be able to look to, and learn from, other Indigenous-led, community-engaged collaborative research projects that focus on the legacies of the Canadian government's policies for Indigenous populations. For instance, the Assiniboia Indian Residential School Legacy Group partnered with an academic team from the

University of Manitoba on a community-driven initiative that resulted in a book about survivor experiences presented alongside memories of Winnipeg residents, school staff, and others.[42] The book *Nii Ndahlohke* is another project that draws on community testimonies and memories, church records, and DIA files to weave together a history of Mount Elgin Residential School (Southern Ontario) that is grounded in Lunaape, the language of the Munsee Delaware. Instructive for our project are the book's academic-community collaboration and use of accessible language for public readership.[43] Similarly, the Manitoba Indigenous Tuberculosis History Project is an ongoing, years-long research project with First Nations, Inuit, and Métis people who were treated for tuberculosis in Manitoba between the 1930s and the 1970s. This work involves efforts to return photographs from official repositories such as the Manitoba Lung Association and Library and Archives Canada to families and communities for naming and re-interpretation.[44]

Reclaiming Stories, Restor(y)ing Self and Community

Though it is difficult for them to tell aspects of their stories, each Black Hawk understands the importance of the visibility of such stories. Chris explained why he testified for the Truth and Reconciliation Commission in his second language: "I had heard that a lot of Canadians had never heard about residential schools, so when I had a chance to testify, I made sure that it was not in the native language so that Canadians in general would understand what I was saying. It's all in English." During Alexandra and Chris' last meeting, Chris expressed his hope that this project could help increase awareness and understanding of the effects of residential school on the survivors and their communities.

Kelly described how talking about his time at school can be unsettling, but he does so in order for the public to understand what it was really like to attend residential school. He explained that when the book has been completed, "I want to be able to walk away and say, 'You know, I've done my best to educate the public about what happened to me.'" Although David struggles with the memories of what happened while at residential school, he walked for three and a half months to raise awareness about residential school abuse and as part of his own healing journey. To David, these stories have to continue to be shared so that the younger generations never forget the journeys that brought them to today, nor the memories of the Elders who cared for them when they were children. Although these troubling and traumatic pasts cannot be changed, "that does not mean history is static and dead. History is alive. It needs recognition and attention."[45] One community Elder working with the research team in Australia captured the importance of using the past to restore and promote well-being in the present in stating that "our history is our healing."[46]

Beyond returning, or repatriating, the photographs themselves, our project with the Black Hawks is a repatriation of the narrative about a time period and event that so defined their early lives: the 1951 hockey season and the team's famous Southern Ontario tour. This history is "returned" both to them and to their communities, and the right to tell their own story is firmly in their hands. In this way, we expand what has been termed "visual repatriation" to mean returning the power to tell stories in ways that make sense to community members, similar to what Indigenous researcher Jeff Corntassel calls "restory."[47]

Indigenous scholar Qwul'sih'yah'maht (Robina Thomas) explains the importance of a restorying-based approach for work with residential school survivors: "Every time someone who went to residential school dies without telling his or her stories, our government and the churches look more innocent. Telling these stories is a form of resistance to colonization."[48] One of the Elders of the Truth and Reconciliation Commission's Survivors Circle, Dr. Barney Williams, expressed a similar sentiment about the significance of telling his and the other survivors' stories. He explained that through the witnessing process, "the voices of the unheard became heard."[49] Restorying is deeply linked to homeland, family, and restitution for the injustices of the past.

Indigenous counter-narratives, as a restorying force, can challenge Canada's self-congratulatory view of a history that began with white settlement. A restorying approach also involves merging narratives of Indigenous resilience, like those of the Black Hawks, into "the public remembering of a contested past."[50] According to Indigenous philosopher Aküm Longchari, who hails from a region near India, restorying can be thought of as re-establishing a people's rightful space in history and has been called "the deeper challenge of peacebuilding."[51]

For the former Black Hawks, restorying these photographs helps them to build and tell a narrative about their experiences as a Black Hawk in a way that makes sense for them, their families, and their communities. Restorying becomes a *restoring* of the boys' humanity that envisions Indigenous survival into the future. The Black Hawks' engagement with the photographs, taken of them without their permission and used to promote the very system that tried to strip away their identities, gives the images and the narrative surrounding them new meaning and purpose. Nearing the end of his life, Kelly has said that more and more he finds himself back at the beginning, trying to understand colonization and what led to the creation of the residential school system. He wonders why Indigenous Peoples are still fighting the same battles for rights that they have been since he was a young man, and sometimes wonders if their efforts are fruitless. Yet he cannot help but be hopeful about this project.

CHAPTER 2

THE TRUTH ABOUT PHOTOGRAPHS

Photographing Indigenous People: An Exploitative History

Scholars who research Indian residential schools have come to understand that photographs of children at these institutions can hide as much as they reveal.[1] While the subject matter captured in these photos, like students in a classroom, might appear commonplace or even innocent, it is important to approach residential school photographs with a critical eye while remembering that these pictures usually served a bigger purpose. Photographs of sports, like the ones taken of the Black Hawks, must be approached the same way, and are best understood within the long history of outsiders taking photographs of Indigenous and other non-white groups to support a political or ideological agenda. Consider: what might pictures of smiling, neatly outfitted Indigenous boys playing Canada's beloved game of hockey have suggested to newspaper readers in the 1920s? Or the 1950s? Or even the 1980s, before the last Indian residential school closed? Photographs, specifically those taken for official reporting purposes, are not harmless snapshots capturing a special moment in time; they are often overt propaganda.

The set of photographs of the Black Hawks taken by the Division in 1951, which was sponsored by the DIA, fit into three important contexts: 1) British imperialists' tendency, in the nineteenth and early twentieth centuries, to record their expansionist dreams by taking photographs of Indigenous and other non-white peoples whose lands they aimed to acquire and control; 2) the Canadian government's use of photography to visually demonstrate their right to rule Indigenous lands and promote white settlement; and 3) photographic archives of students at Indian residential schools in Canada and the United States.

It seems unimaginative to say we need to "dive below the surface" of what is first seen in a photograph, but the truth is, photographs are powerful conveyers of meaning that go well beyond the contents they depict, which makes analyzing those messages crucial. A picture of Indigenous boys from a residential school playing hockey is never just about hockey; it is also about progress and assimilation, cultural transformation, white settlement, and Canadian nation-building. Or it is about survival and pleasure—depending on who is looking. The English language is filled with metaphors that alert us to the power of imagery and the need to take that power seriously: "There is more than what meets the eye" means that something under consideration has unknown qualities that require further investigation. "Appearances can be deceptive" cautions us to be aware of our immediate surroundings. If something is "more than it appears to be," we need to understand what else it could be. Perhaps it is something misleading.

When looking at a photograph, especially professionally taken photographs, it is crucial to consider: For whom is the photographer working? To whom might they be planning to sell this image? What type of equipment did they use? What is the audience meant to see, or take no notice of? How are the people reacting to being photographed?[2] Consider other vital details. Who are the people being photographed? Whose names are identified? When and where was the photograph taken? What was happening more broadly in society that the people in the photograph would have been aware of? Trying to answer these questions about photographs helps us to understand how images have "a more or less hidden agenda" and emphasizes the "need to keep reminding ourselves that (photographs) are cultural artifacts no more 'natural' than any other."[3]

Since the emergence of photography, Europeans and their institutions have used this technology to define, measure, and objectify Indigenous and other non-white communities. The people behind the camera could have been missionaries, explorers, anthropologists, government officials, teachers, traders, and others. The academic discipline of anthropology—the scientific study of humans—played an especially key role in transmitting ideas about far-off peoples and cultures to the European public. During the Victorian period, from the 1830s to 1901, Europe underwent a technological revolution. For educated people, the mindset of the era dictated that new scientific instruments could solve "the problem of objectivity."[4] The camera was considered the pinnacle of a neutral, scientific approach. For anthropologists and other academics during this period, photography was a crucial component of their work. The fact that photography was seen as an objective medium added to the photographs' authority, cemented further by the "collection, display and discipline" involved.[5]

Since photos were produced mechanically and were seen as the height of modern technology in the nineteenth and early twentieth centuries, what was photographed had an air of authority and was regarded as "the truth" instead of as a representation.[6] Even though photographs were often staged with props, or the participants posed to convey a certain message to viewers, photography proved to be a highly convincing tool.[7] Photography was, in short, mistakenly regarded as "a purveyor of truth and the ideal medium to document history."[8] In only rare cases were Indigenous Peoples themselves the photographers.[9] Two researchers who partnered with the Kainai Nation in present-day southern Alberta on a visual repatriation project centred on photographs taken by an anthropologist in the 1920s explain the consequences of photographs taken by outsiders: "The vast majority of photographs of First Nations people have depicted them as non-Natives wanted to see them, and from a position of relative ignorance of Native cultures."[10]

Photography was the ideal vehicle for capturing and communicating the lifeways of "peoples who would shortly disappear forever" to European armchair travellers.[11] While paintings were widely understood to be mere representations, the camera was seen as a "truth-teller."

Simply put, "images were a powerful means of communicating ideas about Indigenous peoples."[12] European photographers captured colourful cultural rites such as the high jumping of the Tutsis, a Rwandan ethnic group. Written representations of such events were seen as inadequate by comparison.[13] By reproducing an image of a cultural "Other" from a far-off part of the world, viewers trusted that the photographer had ensured the realism of the subject(s).

Much of the photography from this period emphasized cultural difference: the (perceived) distinctions between the dominant European society and the non-white peoples of the world who were thought to be vanishing forever. This period was the height of social Darwinian ideas that (mis)characterized Indigenous and other non-European peoples as dying races bound for extinction. Photography furthered this racist notion by seeming to confirm various racial "types" or "specimens" of the non-Western world, playing into the anthropological debates of the mid-nineteenth century, when questions of race took centre stage.[14] The different racial "types" were classified by observable and measurable physical characteristics that were thought to indicate the group's place in an evolutionary hierarchy.[15] White people were considered to be the highest form of civilization. Many "scientific" efforts at documenting Indigenous cultures through visual methods were driven by the belief that their societies were in decline due to the advancement of civilization.[16]

One of the most frequently used tools in the anthropologist's newly scientific toolbox was anthropometry—the measurement of different racial "types" for later classification—which was established in the late 1850s. Researchers saw photography as a natural way of capturing what were perceived to be essential physical differences of Indigenous and other non-European peoples. One scholar explains how anthropometry and photography fit together: "By visualizing non-Western peoples through anthropometric photography, it was thought anthropologists could extract objective scientific data that would shed light on the origins and development of humankind. Illustrating the classification and ordering of peoples . . . these photographs also preserved for the future a record of the 'vanishing' races."[17] You are probably familiar with anthropometric photographs without even realizing it. These are photos that appear standard in format; for instance, each member of a village having been photographed head-on and again from the side, sometimes with a measuring stick visible in the picture. The standardization of these images suggested a type of scientific catalogue which seemed to lend credibility to the researcher's "findings."[18] Measurements and other data were often recorded separately from the pictures yet designed to be interpreted together.[19] For example, the anthropologist who photographed the Kainai in Alberta in the 1920s also took hair samples from them.[20]

Photographs of Indigenous and non-white peoples were taken for both "scientific" and commercial purposes, though photographs intended for research often also ended up in the commercial realm. Through reprinting, "academic" portraits were commonly converted into popular formats.[21] These images made their way to different corners of the globe: "thousands of ethnographic photographs . . . [were circulated] as postcards, exhibited in the great international exhibitions, and collected by museums across the world."[22] The postcard "Indian Braves, Calgary, Alta." from the early 1900s (Figure 2), taken by a commercial photographer, illustrates how the anthropometric "academic" style also found its way into postcards.

It is also worth considering the impact of early photographic technology on the images themselves. For example, before 1884, negatives made of thick glass were used instead of paper-roll film.[23] Each negative weighed almost a pound. A photographer would need a wagonload's worth of chemicals, a dark tent, and a large camera apparatus in addition to the glass negatives. During the exposure period, which lasted several minutes, the individual being photographed had to keep perfectly still—at times, a metal vise was employed and disguised by later painting over it after the image was developed. The fact that those photographed had to sit stock-still for minutes, often in positions not of their choosing, has important implications for viewing pictures from this time period: "[The] limitation of equipment should be taken into consideration when one views posed, 'stoic' portraits of Indians. Not until later did more portable, faster-speed equipment allow for the

Figure 2. This photo postcard from 190-? demonstrates how the academic "anthropometric" style of photographing Indigenous Peoples sometimes made its way into commercially produced photographs. In turn, these photographs had a wide reach as postcards. Published by D.J.Y. Co. Ltd., Calgary, Alta.; Warwick Bros. and Rutter, Limited, Printers, Toronto. Public domain.

spontaneity of everyday behavior to be captured."[24] Understanding the circumstances surrounding the photographs is thus crucial; what has become a stereotype, the stoic—or unemotional—Indigenous person, could very well have been influenced by the technological limitations of photography during the mid-to-late 1800s.

Basic details about Indigenous culture, such as clothing and adornments, were also misrepresented in some Native American photography during this period. Sometimes the visual deception hinged on clothing the photographic subjects in garments that might have been recognizably "Indian" in a broad sense, but were culturally inaccurate, such as some of the photographs that were taken during the Colorado River Expedition of 1871–1873. It was later revealed that the buckskin clothing worn in the photographs had been made to order for the expedition based on old patterns.[25] More overt "costuming" can be seen in a photograph from about 1900, in which the Indigenous man photographed is surrounded by artifacts that have visible museum catalog tags. Another modification that was sometimes made to photographs in the name of "authenticity" was the addition of body paint in post-production.[26]

Historical accuracy was clearly not the photographers' main objective. Seattle photographer Edward Curtis, who would go on to publish a famous series of photographs called *The North American Indian from 1907 to 1930*, attempted to situate his images in a long-gone time. One researcher has argued, "His photographs were tiny time machines intended to take the viewer back before history began into a romantic world of a technologically primitive people. Any evidence of contact with white culture contaminated this image."[27]

Historical photographs of Indigenous and other colonized peoples, consequently, should not be viewed as capturing an actual past reality. Rather, they represent a past *symbolic* reality. Brown et al. explain this distinction very clearly: "Photographs of First Nations people therefore need to be understood as being about the problematic relationship between Native and non-Native peoples as much as they were about the details recorded [in the image]."[28]

All of these examples serve to remind the viewer that historical photographs of Indigenous people must be interpreted cautiously, contextually, and in combination with other data sources. What might be the purpose, then, of examining these inaccurate photographs? One researcher suggests "the value of these North American Indian photographs then is primarily that they reveal how American photographers, even anthropologists, distorted the view of Indians for commercial, aesthetic or other purposes."[29]

In photographs of Indigenous people, regardless of their purpose, those photographed tended to conform to stereotypes: the Romantic, the Warlike, the Vanishing, and the Noble Savage.[30] In fact, the photo that opened Curtis's multi-volume series was given the straightforward title "The Vanishing Race." In case the readers had any doubt, Curtis explained "that Indians as a race . . . are passing into the darkness of an unknown future."[31] To emphasize the differences between mainstream society and Indigenous lives, photographers relied on known visual conventions to communicate messages to the observer: "The clothes and ornaments worn by First Nations people in historic photographs (hide or cloth; moccasins or shoes) conveyed messages readily understood within the dominant society."[32] For instance, a photograph featuring Indigenous people with short hair and Western clothing promised that assimilation was successfully underway. This was also a common photographic approach for photographs of students at Indian schools, as we will see later in this chapter. Imagery featuring Indigenous people in traditional regalia conformed to the stereotype of the Noble Savage and, perhaps, signalled what could be lost when Indigenous people eventually "vanished."

Picturing Modern Canada

It is important to understand the Canadian government's history of photographic propaganda because, as co-administrators with the major Christian churches, they had a central role in the Indian residential school system. The Canadian government has long used photographs to further nation-building objectives, the fact of which emphasizes how photography is not neutral but can be used for political or ideological purposes.[33] Governments also use(d) visual methods for discipline and surveillance, usually with the justification that such technologies are for the "greater good." Video surveillance of protestors is a modern-day example, though the use of photographs for mug shots can be traced as far back as the 1880s in Paris.[34]

Though not overtly focused on discipline, past photographic practices of the Canadian government exerted control in their own way. Researchers have argued that photographing Indigenous people enacted a kind of indirect, though highly important, control via how their communities were represented. Photo-stories that feature representations of the Arctic and Subarctic from the Division taken between 1955 and 1971 helped to reinforce the public's perception of the Canadian government as a "caretaker" of Northern Indigenous Peoples, who were regularly presented as a homogeneous group and often not individually named.[35] The Division, which produced the photo-stories that appeared regularly in Canadian media as well as the Black Hawks tour images, was tightly connected to the federal government's agenda that during the late 1950s and 1960s included exploiting the natural resources of the far North.[36]

Photographs were used to promote white settlement on former Indigenous-controlled lands.[37] Photographs of growing towns, new industries, and transportation methods like the railway helped to convince potential settlers to move west. The photographs of recent European arrival Arthur Rafton-Canning portrayed what he considered to be great achievements of modernity and efficiency in the settlement and development of Alberta, an area that had only recently been brought under the full control of the Canadian government.[38] He photographed new agricultural machinery, the Lethbridge viaduct, and—of course—the railway. After the city became a major railway hub, the marketing of images of Indigenous Peoples who had lived on the prairies before European settlement became more and more popular.

Viewers wanted a glimpse into the lives of "authentic" Plains (or prairie) Indigenous groups.[39] Rafton-Canning's photographs were probably sold as postcards and souvenirs. His photographs, like those of Edward Curtis, showed settler society and First Nations, such as local Niitsitapi, as occupying "opposite poles of the development spectrum."[40] Images of Indigenous people wearing traditional garments showing a "primitive" way of life captured a supposedly dying culture in contrast to the modern Canadian state. That settlers would have had little direct contact with Indigenous people only served to heighten their status as "exotic." In the absence of actual interaction between settlers and Indigenous people, photography was influential in shaping mainstream society's perceptions about Indigenous lives and futures.

Photographs suggested to potential prairie settlers, for example, that their growing villages, towns, and cities had the proper institutions for advanced society: new hospitals, shops with modern wares, a fire station, and public schools. The promotional pamphlets that included these pictures also provided visual reassurance that the "problems" of early settlement were taken care of. Pictures of the Brandon Indian Residential School in Brandon, Manitoba, appeared in booklets[41] that promoted the region to white settlers in the early 1900s, serving to confirm that the region's Indigenous inhabitants no longer posed a threat to European settlement and that Indigenous children were being properly assimilated. In accordance with photographic conventions of the period, the photographs of this school emphasize the imposing physical structures and expansive campuses that seem to represent the order and discipline that students would learn on-site. The reality "behind" these images has now been well-documented. These buildings were usually poorly constructed and what passed for instilling discipline into its Indigenous residents was a system of forced physical labour that contributed to students' poor health and early deaths.[42]

In another souvenir photo book from the same period in Brandon, printed in 1901, out of twelve total photographs one is of a large grouping of Indigenous people.[43] About a dozen adults are visible in "Indians at the Fair," with most on horseback in what appears to be ceremonial attire. Two older Indigenous men kneel at the forefront wearing a combination of Western and Indigenous clothing, surrounding what appears to be a drum. A white man in a suit and hat stands next to a third elderly Indigenous man (Figure 3). This photograph is the book's only image that contains people shown at any discernible size. In the other photographs, the emphasis is clearly on the amenities that the growing city had on offer: stately buildings, residential streetscapes, numerous church denominations, and transportation via railway. In one photo, a flotilla of logs on the Assiniboine River suggests that industry and opportunity await.

What, then, could it mean that a photograph of "Indians at the Fair" had been included as the final image in this *Photographic View Album*? At first glance, a modern viewer could wonder if the white man is a local Indian Agent who has coerced a local First Nation into a public performance. After all, it was not until 1914 that the Indian Act began to restrict Indigenous people from performing off-reserve

Figure 3. This photo, c. 1901, is from the souvenir photo book *Photographic View Album of Brandon, MB.* Published by W.G. MacFarlane for D.E. Clement, Toronto. Used with permission from the National Gallery of Canada, which holds the original.

in traditional clothing, though even then exceptions were made if the Superintendent of the DIA or the local Indian Agent gave their permission. Alternatively, the white man could have been a promoter or manager of the event itself, and, knowing how popular "Indian" displays were with the public, arranged for one of the local nations—perhaps the nearby Wipazoka Wakpa (Sioux Valley Dakota Nation)—to attend.

It would be overly simplistic to conclude from the photograph that the dynamics surrounding their participation were wholly exploitative. More investigation into the historical context of the photograph reveals both nuances and contradictions about Indigenous people's participation in such events in the early 1900s and sheds light on why such an image might have been included in a souvenir photo-book. One account of how local Indigenous groups came to perform explains: "The Brandon Fair never fails to invite the Indians under this Agency to take part in these Attractions. A large tent and space is provided to show the interested and curious Whites at 25 cents each."[44] Indigenous groups used these profits to cover costs and to improve their "costumes" (properly known as regalia). Researchers further explain that, significantly, Indigenous Peoples also saw an opportunity in these performances to continue ceremonial practices that had been formally forbidden[45] as well as to meet people from other Indigenous communities. However, these gatherings and performances were highly embarrassing to the DIA's officials, who feared that photographs of "the Indians in war paint and feathers will be pictured in the English and American journals" and give the impression that those in charge of settling Canada's West had failed in "taming" its original inhabitants.[46]

Such exhibits of Indigenous performances were enormously popular during this era. Their sheer popularity might, in fact, be the most plausible explanation for the photograph in the Brandon souvenir book. It suggested to readers that settlers to Brandon (and, by extension, the West) would be promised these types of "exotic" encounters. The fact that the image was noted to be from "the Fair" could have also reassured viewers that seeing Indigenous people in ceremonial garments—which suggested primitiveness—was reserved for extraordinary events and was not a part of everyday life in modernizing, industrializing Canada. Such threats to the safety of settlers to the region were, after all, not so distant; in 1895, newspapers reported that an armoured regiment of the Canadian army, the Royal Canadian Dragoons, was ready to "guard the Manitoba boundary against the invasions of half-breeds and Indians" from North Dakota.[47] All of these possible explanations, both for the photograph itself and for its inclusion in the book of photographs, serve to emphasize the importance of understanding the historical, socio-cultural, and political circumstances surrounding photographs of Indigenous Peoples in Canada, as well as their implications.

Photographing Indigenous Children at School

British imperialists used photography in "calculated and sophisticated ways" to document the progress being made at boarding and missionary schools for Indigenous and Black students around the world.[48] In Freetown, capital of the then British colony Sierra Leone, professional photographers in the 1890s captured an image of a graduating class of Fourah Bay College. All graduates wore academic caps and gowns, signifiers of European educational achievement.[49] These graduates were probably the first generation of children born to emancipated enslaved persons who were brought as settlers to Sierra Leone via British humanitarian and abolitionist initiatives. A second photo taken in South Africa's British Cape Colony in the 1870s captures a similar scene with younger Black boys in Victorian suits. By educating these sons of chiefs, the Anglican Church and British government hoped that the graduates would bring "civilization" and Christianity back to their communities of origin.[50]

"Before and after" pictures were common in both the American and Canadian Indian school contexts. Administrators of Indian education used them as a subtle but effective publicity tool that also reinforced common racial stereotypes.[51] For instance, there is a well-known 1897 picture set of student Thomas Moore Keesick "before" entering Regina Indian Industrial School, in Indigenous dress and holding a toy pistol, and "after," slightly older, uniformed in Western clothing and with his hair cut short. These photographs appeared together in the DIA Annual Report in 1896 and suggested that he was a success story of assimilation thanks to his time at residential school, perhaps now on his way to take his proper place as a farmer or a worker in a factory. However, these photographs obscured the truth about his life, about the residential school system, and about the government and churches' broader objectives for Indigenous people. According to the best available records, Keesick died at the age of twelve, having been sent home from school to his reserve ill with tuberculosis.[52] Researchers of residential schools use this example to emphasize the importance of understanding how these photographs could be used to steer attention towards, and also away from, important information.

In North America, residential school (or boarding school, to use the American term) photography conveyed multiple messages to funders, administrators, and the public. These images were "powerful vehicles of ideology"[53] that emphasized the "civilizing" process promoted by government- and church-run institutions.[54] The most common photos from American boarding schools are of organized sports and band practices, which provided visual evidence for white viewers that Native American children were being appropriately civilized and socialized.[55] For the American and Canadian public during these time periods, "Native dress"—the clothes that Indigenous children would likely have been wearing upon their arrival at school—symbolized the "backwardness" of traditional customs. This association was so strong that returning to traditional ways was referred to as "going back to the blanket."[56] Given the links, then, between physical appearance and successful adoption of white culture, producing images of children who had seemingly shed the trappings of their previous lives would have been paramount for the public, government officials, and church audiences.

Photographs of Indigenous children wearing Euro-Canadian clothing and engaging in mainstream recreational activities served as advertisements for assimilation, with the medium of hockey—in the case of the Black Hawks—adding an extra layer of meaning. Hockey had, and continues to have, a role in defining "who was Canadian and who was less (or not) Canadian."[57] By the Second World War, hockey was firmly associated with whiteness and middle-class masculinity,[58] and by the time the Black Hawks set off for Southern Ontario in 1951, organized youth hockey for boys was immensely popular. Sport was thought to promote character development and citizenship for Canada's young people, and minor hockey was a particularly good vehicle for developing proper masculinity in boys.[59]

When the Black Hawks hit the ice, then, they were participating in a universally recognizable ritual of Canadian boyhood, "the great Canadian game,"[60] photos of which appeared weekly in sports sections of local and national newspapers. Audience members and the Canadian public who would become acquainted with the story of the Black Hawks through the tour's expansive media coverage would not only see the polite, clean-playing boys as examples of the potential for Indigenous people to assimilate into Canadian society, but also of the success of the Anglican residential schooling program.

CHAPTER 3

PROMOTING THE "GOOD WORK" OF SCHOOLING

After the Second World War, every Canadian had a role to play in ensuring a unified citizenry fit for defending the country and meeting the challenges of modern society. This included the Black Hawks. Carefully regulated recreation, the thinking went, would avoid young Canadians diverging from accepted norms. Crucially, it would also help to instill middle-class, Anglo-Saxon values, such as the value of hard work. According to the prevailing stereotypes about Indigenous Peoples, they required strict guidance in both work and play. "It would appear," wrote the Saskatchewan Regional Supervisor of Indian Agencies about a 1948 proposal to allow residential school students to enroll beyond Grade 8, "that much of the hope for success lies in the right kind of discipline, with competent instruction both during the study hours and during recreation."[1]

Policy changes had helped to reshape opportunities for physical culture—especially competitive sports—in the postwar era of residential schooling, but attention to the importance of sports and games for character development had long been a part of residential schools. Administrators hoped that physical activities emphasizing desired character attributes, such as discipline and hard work, would lead to transformations in other areas of school life, such as classroom work. In particular, the use of recreation in Anglican schools was designed to promote discipline, team spirit, and patriotism.[2] The Indian and Eskimo Residential Schools Commission, which oversaw the administration of the Anglican Indian residential schools, advised teachers to incorporate supervised play and recreation into their daily curriculum to teach students how to "play the game" properly and, by extension, how to use their leisure time wisely.[3]

The DIA wanted the education system to develop a desirable ethical framework in the students, and they instructed teachers to use physical education to educate students on "the spirit of fair play" as part of students' overall moral development,[4] a tactic that was also common in the public school system at the time. In particular, the DIA believed that "running, jumping, ball games and similar sports are vitally important as a means of molding the child's character and for general exercise."[5]

Administrators were also attracted to the potential of sport to be used as a public relations tool in the residential school system. At Kamloops Indian Residential School in British Columbia, for instance, the dance troupes and brass bands probably served as showpieces to rally public support behind the institution.[6] When describing the boys' military band's successful performance for visiting dignitaries, Lebret Indian Residential School's principal in Saskatchewan reflected on the important role of public-facing school programs. He described that in their public performance, the schoolboys "are very popular and sympathetic and I think it constitutes such a good advertisement for the efforts we do in the School to civilize them."[7] From his statement, it is clear the Indian residential school officials understood the publicity value of student exhibitions, especially—it seemed—ones where students were shown to be excelling in Euro-Canadian forms of disciplined recreation.

A parallel could be found in Native American boarding schools to the south, where, from the late 1800s to the 1930s, school administrators used the cultural prominence of sport and the importance of sport in American education to advance their own agendas. The big-time sports events of some American residential schools pitted Native American students against white students in popular sporting competitions to demonstrate the effects of the boarding school system. Haskell boarding school's homecoming for their famous football team of the 1920s is one example of a high-profile sporting event that school officials promoted through an extensive marketing campaign.[8] In another example, the principals at the Sherman Institute used sport marketing to enhance the school's reputation, selling the school as the best training ground for civilizing Native Americans.[9] Similar messages were evident in the Canadian residential school system.

Redefining Indigenous understandings of gender was an important element of physical education. The activities permitted and promoted by the schools attempted to reinforce Euro-Canadian gender roles. The pursuit of physical fitness for manual labour or the development of "masculine" character traits, such as courage, toughness, and a Protestant work ethic, were the intended effects of training for boys. Activities for boys were to be active, vigorous, and strenuous, while girls were provided with activities that aimed to teach them to be passive, see themselves as fragile, and be cooperative rather than competitive. School administrators favoured gentle exercises for girls, like walking, skating, and swimming, and non-physical recreation such as playing with dolls. Sports, drills, and strength and fitness exercises were usually reserved for boys.[10] For example, at Brandon Residential School the principal's request for sports equipment included skates and hockey sticks for the boys but only skates for the girls.[11] Boys could often move about the residential school properties with relative freedom, whereas the girls were watched over carefully. In Alberta, the recollections of one former supervisor at Morley Residential School from the interwar period describe how a female staff member chaperoned the girls' walks or games while the boys "are free to roam where they wish."[12] The belief in appropriate gender roles was so strongly embedded within the actions of the staff that ideas about proper male and female behaviour were simply taken for granted.[13] Also in Alberta, according to Principal Naessens of the High River Industrial School (also known as Dunbow or St. Joseph's), writing in 1900, while the boys had successful football and hockey teams ("a great factor in the training of our boys"), the girls "indulge in more moderate exercises."[14]

Naessens's proclamations echoed observers' remarks from previous decades, indicating that connections between sports and character formation for Indigenous adolescents, especially for boys, were an enduring belief. Principal Motion remarked positively on his male students' successes in the "manly sports" of football, baseball, and basketball in his 1904 report on the Alberni Boarding School in British Columbia.[15] The previous year, writing in the *National Monthly of Canada*, a visitor to Elkhorn Indian Residential School in present-day Manitoba commended the joint DIA–church policy of physical education in residential schools. Of the obviously masculine athlete, she wrote: "To carry a football down the field past all his antagonists . . . requires courage, self-reliance, and strenuousness."[16] There seemed to be no limit to what imagined improvements Euro-Canadian sports could inspire. Drawing on familiar discourses that suggested sports, if properly overseen, could mould boys into men of good character, the reporter concluded that "the Indian who can run up against a white rival on the field and hold his own, will be all the better for it when he comes to face him as a competitor in the sterner affairs of life."[17]

By the late 1940s, it was clear to the officials at the DIA that a program of physical education that included Euro-Canadian sports and games could help move its agenda along.[18] Federal officials believed that, in addition to being a cost-effective solution for dealing with the poor health conditions in the schools, organized sports and games would facilitate the integration of Indigenous youth into the public school system by teaching them the physical competencies that youth in the public school system were already mastering. Federal officials also believed that sports and games would help smooth the progress of Indigenous assimilation into broader Canadian society by bringing Indigenous and non-Indigenous people into contact with each other through competition.

The boys of the Black Hawks indeed attended residential school during a key period of policy change at the DIA. The Department of National Health and Welfare was created in 1945 with the goal of improving Canadians' health through physical fitness.[19] In the mid-1940s, the DIA also undertook new directions in its programs. It had asked for direct feedback from its Indian Agents—an unusual move—and determined that the worrying trend of rising Indigenous activism could be quashed through increased contact with whites ("integration"), increased educational opportunities and the establishment of sports and sports clubs, particularly at the federally-run residential and day schools.[20] Gifford Swartman, the Indian Agent for the catchment area of Pelican Lake who would come to play a key role in establishing the Black Hawks, suggested in his feedback to headquarters that student participation in "athletic and other forms of recreation" at school would lead to the values that sport promoted—such as health and disciplined use of leisure time—also being adopted on the reserves. Such participation would promote the "[beneficial] and civilizing effects of organized sports and games, especially the amateur kind," in the words of one scholar. [21]

From a policy-administrative standpoint, the 1947 merger of the Canadian Citizenship Branch and the DIA into a joint Department of Citizenship and Immigration spoke volumes about the government's citizenship aspirations for Indigenous people.[22] This move was more than just an administrative reshuffle. In 1950, Prime Minister St. Laurent explained that his rationale for the merger had been twofold: to assimilate new arrivals to the country and "to make Canadian citizens of as many as possible of the descendants of the original inhabitants of this country."[23]

The Department of Citizenship and Immigration focused on integrating new immigrants into mainstream Canadian life through education and "citizenship training" programs that were also extended to Indigenous Peoples. Canadian immigrants, however, had more leeway to negotiate the terms of their Canadianization. Policies towards Indigenous Peoples were notably more focused on assimilation. While Indigenous Peoples might be able to retain some superficial cultural distinctiveness, for instance the Black Hawks giving lacrosse sticks to competing teams on their hockey tour,[24] "citizenship campaigns also demand[ed] conformity to dominant norms. . . . [o]fficials, experts, and volunteers intended that, like their immigrant counterparts, Aboriginal youth and adults would adopt Canadian social mores."[25] This new direction signalled a type of integration for Indigenous Peoples through which they would become just another ethnic minority in the country's growing cultural mosaic. Indigenous Peoples were viewed as similar to recent immigrants who required special training to become Canadian.[26] Yet even after the mid-century merger of the Canadian Citizenship Branch and the DIA, there was little overt change in terms of policy: assimilation, now referred to as citizenship education, remained the overall objective.[27]

The rapid expansion of residential school sports teams across the country became a critical extension of the new policy emphasis on integration.[28] However, not just any sports or physical activities would do, as the following example from the Jan Eisenhardt Fonds at Western University shows. Eisenhardt was the first supervisor of physical education and recreation at the DIA. Although he was employed there for only a short period of time, from 1950 to 1951, he amassed a large archival collection, among which is a single photo of a person in ceremonial potlatch attire accompanied by the comment, "*Potlatch costume.* We would like to change this to more wholesome *community activities*" (emphasis in original). In the eyes of the DIA, sports and recreational activities had to fit into Euro-Canadian frameworks to be seen as valid and worthwhile endeavours.

The DIA provided additional financial support to day and residential schools that fostered competitive opportunities involving both Indian and public schools and encouraged Indigenous athletes to play on local non-Indigenous teams and leagues.[29] Stories of these activities were recorded from time to time in various local newspapers. In 1951, the *Sault Daily Star* reported that Eisenhardt had successfully negotiated with the Sault Ste. Marie city council to have one of its recreation directors spend two days per week during the summer at the Garden River First Nation Reserve, located a few miles east of the city. To Eisenhardt, the arrangement would benefit the people from both Garden River and Sault Ste. Marie. "The Indian people's contact was with the wrong type of white man," he explained; "from contact with city children in an organized recreation scheme, the reserve children would learn a great deal of good. The city would benefit by getting better future citizens."[30] The fact that the DIA would cover the costs of the additional programming was an incentive that made the program more attractive. In response to Eisenhardt, Alderman Peter King emphasized the economic benefits of the deal, stating that such a simple plan "would make the children better citizens at no cost to the city."[31]

In the *Indian School Bulletin* (the *Bulletin*), a circular newsletter that the DIA sent to all its teachers, physical activities were explained as an effective way to impose a subtle form of discipline. One article, written by a DIA agent, explained that efforts to teach Indigenous youth about "the working aspects of life" needed to be enhanced with proper physical activity programs. "It should not be forgotten that people must also play," the writer advised. Teachers needed to understand that "recreation and relaxation lead to a variety of associations and group activities which educate the whole man." It would therefore be "essential that the youth in school and out of it, should have opportunities for physical exercise and recreation. Sports, games and recreation provide the means; where traditional forms are lacking, new ones can be introduced."[32] Throughout the years, the *Bulletin* made much of the notion that "fun" should be emphasized in devising activities. Sometimes the framing took the form of a directive: "It is important that a gay and happy atmosphere prevails. Give the pupils a chance to keep in contact with the outside world either by sending teams to competitions or bringing teams to the school to compete on home grounds."[33]

The ideal sport and recreation program imposed a structured schedule, was dependent on the authority of a formally trained instructor, and included activities that brought Indigenous youth into contact with white citizens. Teachers and Indian Agents were to encourage residential school graduates to develop and lead programs on reserves, using organized sports especially to foster interactions between Indigenous youth and broader society. Readers were told that energetic and friendly competition would help the youth develop a "sense of belonging" that would "contribute directly to making the Indian understand and appreciate the part he ought to play as a citizen of Canada."[34] Sport and recreational activities had to help the church and state fulfill their civilizing and Christianizing agendas, in contrast to what were perceived to be backwards customs, such as the traditional potlatch of Pacific Northwest Indigenous Peoples.

Citizenship education, the thinking went, would prepare students to take up their proper roles in society by teaching them how to think and act in socially acceptable ways. The emphasis on citizenship education was not new and echoed what appeared in public schools.[35] When Eisenhardt resigned from the DIA in November 1951, his parting words highlighted the important contributions that organized physical activity programs were thought to make towards encouraging citizenship values: "I owe much to the cooperation of a growing number of persons who are working for the welfare and advancement of the Indian people, and who appreciate the civic value of a well-planned programme of physical education and recreation. I look forward to seeing the pupils of our Indian schools and the young people of our Indian communities participating more and more with their fellow-Canadians in wholesome activities which afford personal satisfaction and contribute to good citizenship."[36]

Insufficient opportunities for sport and recreation remained common in the residential school system and program delivery was uneven. For instance, officials complained that the residential school at Brandon did not have a gymnasium or recreational hall, while the Portage la Prairie school, also administered by the United Church and relatively close by, did.[37] Brandon Residential School's temporary principal noted in a letter to church headquarters, The Board of Home Missions, that "the church has left [sportsmanship] out of their program too long with evil results."[38]

Photographs of Sports

What was shown in photographs of students at residential schools changed over time, even while the school system's underlying objectives remained largely the same. Take the photographs captured at the Thomas Indian School in Western New York between the 1890s and 1950s: initially, photographs emphasized forced assimilation by showing the children and youth as disciplined workers, but by the 1940s photographs began to demonstrate the more "humane" approach to integration that was popular at the time. For instance, photographs taken during the earlier time span, the forced assimilation period, typically showed students looking stern while working in the field, while photographs taken during the later time span, the "progressive" era, offered depictions of "happy" students engaged in leisure activities like swimming. One of the main messages that we can take away from looking at these pictures, taken over a very long time period, is that photographs express "traces of the belief systems that structure a time and place."[39]

Photographs of residential school students engaged in sports signalled the more "humane" system of assimilation that was present when the Black Hawks undertook their tour of Southern Ontario in 1951. The photographs of the Black Hawks largely conform to the visual conventions of the mid-twentieth century: showing "typical" and contented "Canadian" children enjoying a school-sponsored sports-centred field trip. Furthermore, images of the boys playing the beloved Canadian game of hockey were meant to provide visual evidence of how far Indian schooling had come, and how "civilized" the boys were becoming through their time at school and through spending time in an urban environment visiting institutions like museums and Canada's Parliament.

The NFB photographs of the Black Hawks on tour told a visual story of a natural-seeming transformation: of Indigenous youth into Canadian men. It was also a story of what was *not* present: any traces of their cultural identities as Ojibwe, Anisininew, or Cree persons. The tour photographs seemed to show a seamless process of assimilation, the natural progression from the Doctrine of Discovery to the erasure of Indigenous Peoples as distinct nations.

The photos also demonstrated a romanticized view of Canadian boyhood. "Boyhood" in the decade and a half following the Second World War meant a nostalgic promotion of idealized traits for young males that centred on teamwork, honesty, and emotional fortitude to combat the threat of communism and tyranny from abroad.[40] Photographs of grinning boys in team sport uniforms crowded the sports pages of local newspapers. The Black Hawks' presence in these very sports pages would have been noteworthy, as the press typically took a negative view of Indigenous boys as "unhealthy, intellectually inadequate, delinquent, and in some cases criminal."[41] Working-class and racialized youth came under special scrutiny from the public and the state, perceived as being "even more in need of . . . 'civilizing' and 'Canadianizing' recreation," as scholars explain.[42] The point here for the interpretation of the images of the Black Hawks is that, to the public, male youth hockey was a recognizable vehicle for promoting proper childhood development and would have broadly signalled that the players were undergoing an expected rite of boyhood, perhaps seen as a welcome contrast to how Indigenous boys usually appeared in the public press.

There is an undeniable promotional value of images of Indigenous boys dressed in hockey uniforms, toting familiar equipment, and posing as a team. However, the circulation of images of boys playing hockey at residential schools can set up a type of false similarity between their lives and the lives of white Canadian youth during that era. It can be easy for white Canadians to see the pictures of the Black Hawks and imagine their grandfathers in the boys' place. Seeing something of themselves or their family in these photographs makes the boys' experiences relatable, but it also masks how vastly different life at a residential school was from that of Euro-Canadian children of that generation. Smiling boys in uniform playing on Indian residential school sports teams suggested well-adjusted, healthy, and appropriately socialized male students.[43] Hockey, specifically, is important to Canadian national identity and is viewed as a unifying force across differences. The idealization of the sport has the effect of silencing critics about the destruction that residential schools caused.[44] The reality of residential school sports and its present-day legacy is considerably more complicated than a feel-good hockey narrative.

Images of sports at residential school can be misleading because they *seem* to tell a different story from the one of abuse and cultural removal with which many people are familiar. Photographs of sports suggest they were a trouble-free aspect of the curriculum. While it is true that some students did find sports freeing and a place where they could demonstrate skills equal to—or even better than—their white peers, it would not be correct to assume that being able to participate in sports somehow balanced or "cancelled out" the traumatic experience of residential schooling. The trouble with triumphant sports narratives from Indian schools is that they "can easily mask the fundamental pain and destruction created by assimilation policies."[45]

Sports and physical education at Indian schools were a part of the assimilating agenda of the Canadian government. People who research sport and physical activity see the relationship between the physical body and society as one that, like many other relationships, is influenced by power relations. Therefore, viewers must exercise the same type of caution when looking at photographs of sports at residential schools, as when looking at historical images of Indigenous Peoples generally. Survivor advocate Eugene Arcand, who attended two residential schools in Saskatchewan, provides a vivid example. During a public event in 2016, he explained the story of a photograph of the boys' basketball team from the residential school he attended. Referring to the picture as "staged," he explained why the players' hands could not be seen. All the players had put their hands behind their backs in solidarity with two of their teammates whose hands were severely injured after a beating that had occurred the previous day. The story of the Black Hawks reminds us to look beyond the surface level to the concealed narratives behind the photos and to remember the words of Arcand: "Don't let these pictures fool you because the true story behind them is hurtful."[46]

CHAPTER 4

SURVIVING PELICAN LAKE

It may be tempting to believe that the boys landed at Pelican Lake during the worst possible time to be a residential school student because of the rampant physical abuse and alarming living conditions. The sad reality is that an in-depth look at almost any period over the life of the Canadian residential school system would yield similar results. After spending hundreds of hours scrutinizing government and church archives, it is difficult not to conclude that officials like principals, school inspectors, and Indian Agents engaged in something of a mutual delusion about the system and their roles in it. They convinced themselves, and each other, that conditions were improving, that the new principal they had appointed was surely doing a better job than the last, or that a new group of under-qualified—and sometimes completely unqualified—teachers would finally raise reading levels.

At times things did improve, but then, bound by severe underfunding, general administrative apathy, and little sustained public concern, they returned to a miserable baseline. Therefore, while reading about what life was like for the boys at Pelican Lake during this time period, bear in mind that similar conditions of deprivation existed system-wide for thousands of Indigenous children and youth. Though their tour was unique, the labour to which they were subjected, the abuse they experienced, and the lack of meaningful education they received were not.

It is not an exaggeration to state that, for these survivors, life at residential school was not so different from being in a prison. The Truth and Reconciliation Commission, in fact, explains how residential schools were modelled on schools for delinquent or criminal youth. The treaties that Indigenous nations had entered into, in good faith, had promised on-reserve education. The substandard education that the children received, especially when viewed in combination with the forced labour and neglect that pupils experienced, strikes Kelly as a betrayal of the promises that would have been made to his parents: "Well, I think maybe my parting words from my dad would have been '*Bizindan*. Listen. They're going to teach you.'"

Instead, Indigenous children were more or less hostages of the government, especially after the introduction of the Family Allowance in 1945. The Family Allowance was an income support for families that hinged on obeying certain conditions, such as children attending school.[1] With his characteristic wry humour, Chris pointed out that Premier Leslie Frost was indirectly responsible for him attending school, as it was his government that had introduced the Family Allowance program.

Throughout the course of Canadian history, Indigenous children seem to have been the only ones "who over an extended period of time were required to live in institutions because of their race."[2] As early as the 1940s, Indigenous commentators were making this same point. Métis organizer Malcolm Norris wrote that students who had attended residential schools rightly called them "penitentiaries" and that children "are compelled to attend FOR THE CRIME OF BEING BORN AN INDIAN" (emphasis in original).[3] Some former students who had been sent away to prison schools on account of misbehaviour at Pelican Lake wrote to Indian Agent Gifford Swartman to tell him that they preferred life in their reformatory to their lives at the school. In fact, they recommended that other Pelican Lake students should be sent to join them.[4] It is surely not a coincidence that Chris called the small amount of money he received from the Indian Residential Schools Settlement Agreement a payment for "time served." Kelly compared the way students were forced to improvise to make life at the school bearable to "people making jailbreaks from Alcatraz and the trouble they went through."

A School or a "Workhouse"?

Providing manual labour skills, while also providing resources for the school, was central to the original philosophy of the "half-day system" that was first developed in 1847 and used in Anglican residential schools officially until 1947, after which time it was supposed to have been discontinued—though at some schools it was not.[5] The half-day school policy used in residential schools contributed to students' poor education at Pelican Lake. Older students received a half day of instruction in the classroom, while the other half of the day was spent doing manual labour for the benefit of the school. The origins of the overwork of students in the residential school system can be found in the federal government's inadequate per-student funding model. This model presupposed that the schools would be able to generate income from farming and other endeavours to help offset funding shortfalls.[6] At Pelican Lake and most other schools across Canada, the girls worked by doing the laundry, baking, working in the dairy, sewing, and keeping the dormitories clean and tidy.[7] They also cleaned the dining rooms. In this way, they were trained to be domestic servants and to keep house for their own families once they graduated. In the meantime, they were free labour for the school.

Kelly and Chris have emphasized how the "chores" students did were essential tasks to keep the school functioning on a basic level. It can be a challenge to explain and wrap one's head around just how much work students would have had to undertake to simply keep the school going. Over the course of one long talk with Alexandra, Kelly tried to put into perspective the magnitude of the task, using a present-day hotel chain for comparison. He said, "Can you imagine, like how the Comfort Inns are . . . that would be the size of some of those schools. The work that goes into keeping the Comfort Inn clean and usable for the general public—well, basically, those people that do that kind of work get paid and we didn't."

These basic, unpaid tasks were said to have educational value as "manual training." Students were supposed to learn the importance of hard work, a character trait considered lacking in Indigenous communities, while also being prepared for future employment prospects in Canadian society's serving classes.[8]

The boys at Pelican Lake worked at the school, on its grounds, and beyond. Their farm jobs included the seeding, cultivation, and harvesting of garden produce, as well as learning how to care for the horses, cattle, and pigs.[9] Chris and one of his peers butchered animals for school consumption. The Black Hawks, then age ten to twelve, performed the back-breaking labour of retrieving wood every morning to heat the school. They took a horse-drawn wagon into the woods, a two- or three-mile journey, to fetch the logs from school employee Willie, an elderly Finnish man whose kindness to the boys was a small blessing. This chore was likely part of their supposed training in becoming a "woodsman"—"training" that, not surprisingly, involved clearing brush and removing tree stumps from the school lands.[10] The boys cut and stored seventy tonnes of ice a year for cold storage, which Kelly vividly recalls, and chopped and prepared over eight hundred cords of wood annually to fuel the school furnaces.[11]

A "workhouse" is, in fact, an appropriate way to characterize David, Chris, and Kelly's experience of residential school life. Looking at Figure 4, Kelly reflected on the efforts to clear the wooded land to build the school and farm, with which his father assisted. Kelly's recollections of the labour they undertook as students, however, never fail to mention Willie. Willie would set out early in the morning, travelling from the school to a deep stand of timber, where he would await the arrival of the boys with their horse-drawn sleigh. When Kelly and his fellow students, chilled to the bone, made it to the site where the eight-foot logs were waiting for them, Willie would "have the fire just crackling. 'Oh, I made some tea. Sit down, sit down; sit by the fire and warm up!' and he'd say, 'We've got a couple hours before we start loading the sleigh.'" Reflecting on the reasons behind Willie's actions, Kelly commented, "He was sympathetic. He saw all the bad stuff that was going on. Yeah, oh, Willie. I have fond memories of him."

Figure 4. Looking at this photograph from 194-?, Kelly was prompted to reflect on the labour that had been needed to clear the land to erect the school and all of its buildings. P75-103-S7-125. From the Anglican Church of Canada's Missionary Society of the Church of England in Canada (MSCC) fonds. Reproduced with permission.

Without a doubt, students were used as a workforce to maintain the operation of a school system that deprived the students of their families and of a normal childhood. The volume of work expected from the boys did not go unnoticed. In 1945, Indian Agent Gifford Swartman suggested that the amount of time they spent doing chores reduced the time available for organized sports and games, through which they were to learn important lessons in character development. He thus recommended that Pelican Lake school shift to coal as its fuel source so that more time could be spent pursuing these activities.[12] Chris and Kelly recalled that the coal had to be retrieved from a siding at Pelican Lake's railroad station before shovelling it all into bins or boxes for the school. A few miles from the school each way, this was no small journey.[13]

While the shift to coal might have resulted in a slightly less demanding workday for the boys, they were still relied upon as a main source of labour for the school. In 1951, government officials had to remind the church authorities, who had direct responsibility for the day-to-day workings of the school, that "farming operations . . . [should be conducted] in such a manner that the time and energy of the children are not diverted from whatever academic objectives are proper for the institution."[14] In other words, the government official reprimanded the Pelican Lake administration for continuing to use its students as a labour force. Kelly had two choice words in response to hearing that the students' education was supposed to come first: "That's bullshit." Unsurprisingly, in January 1952 when an engine-room motor failed and could not be quickly repaired, the boys were enlisted at 6:30 a.m. to carry water from the lake to the school for washing and cooking. It was minus twenty degrees.[15]

What did the Black Hawks and other students *learn* at school? In a 1972 interview for his radio show *Our Native Land* on CBC, former Black Hawk Johnny Yesno interviewed Kelly Bull and another schoolmate, Ronald Wesley, for a segment called "The Bad Old Days in Residential School." Johnny recalled how he had to milk cows daily, yet the students themselves were served watered-down milk. Ronald Wesley asked, "If they weren't going to educate the children, why do you move them hundreds of miles just to go and work to keep this building going? They can cut wood at home."[16] In our interview, Chris commented on the school's emphasis on physical labour as a key part of what they learned at school: "We were supposed to be farmers, I guess." Kelly and his family's preferred terminology for what were called "chores" at the time is now "child labour."

Though Chris stated that he felt he had received an "OK" education at Pelican Lake, he had a strong—and, as it turns out, correct—suspicion that he and the other students were being excluded from academic opportunities, such as not getting a say in whether they would attend an academic or technical high school. David, in our interview, recalled his confusion about being sent by the DIA to Thunder Bay from the Shingwauk Indian Residential School in Sault Ste. Marie, where Pelican Lake students were sent for the middle and, for a select few, upper grades, without having graduated from high school: "I wasn't going to school [in Thunder Bay]. I guess they wanted me to play hockey." He guessed—again, correctly—that the DIA would have had to pay for him to keep attending school. Because of his talent and aptitude for hockey, he was sent to Thunder Bay at age sixteen to pursue sports instead. A newspaper article about him and a peer's recent arrival in the city announced the boys' presence and invited potential employers to contact a local citizen who had apparently assumed temporary responsibility for them.[17] David's son, Bradley, today says that the DIA failed his father and that he finds the tour photos of his father being "wined and dined" unsettling.

Kelly admitted to experiencing frustration whenever people suggest that, since he has had a professionally successful life, school could not have been "that bad." Topping the list of resentments about residential school is that he spent his time doing manual labour when he could have received a more advanced academic education. Kelly described how these missed opportunities affected his life; he remarked to the adjudicator at his residential school compensation assessment, "I might have wanted to be a lawyer like yourself. But I couldn't . . . [The lawyer responded]: 'Well, according to your resume, you've done pretty good, Kelly.' And I said, 'Yeah, by whose standards?' . . . the other nagging thing is if I would have had the [lucky] breaks, where the hell would I have been? More opportunities, more education—I might have been further down the road."

Chris had a similar experience at his compensation hearing. He explained that the adjudicators disregarded his experiences of the psychological and emotional trauma of having to "[walk] that tight line all the time, scared to get beat up by my own peers, getting whipped by supervisors." Instead, they homed in on the fact that he learned to speak English fluently, and therefore his experience could not have been that bad.

The education that the children received did not meet provincial standards, nor did students have control over their educational or career paths. A report submitted in 1951, the same year that the Black Hawks undertook their Southern Ontario tour, cautioned that while "the Indians and the general public may suppose that [Pelican Lake and Shingwauk residential schools] conform . . . to the standards and regulations for other schools in Ontario," this assumption should be challenged.[18] In other words, provincial standards were not upheld at either Pelican Lake or Shingwauk, even though the general public and Indigenous communities thought that they were.

In 1951, the Regional Inspector of Indian Schools reported his concerns about student life and facilities at Pelican Lake and Shingwauk Residential Schools. He wrote that the schools compared negatively to the allowances made for those in the Armed Forces, who at least received a special Christmas dinner. Disturbingly, he noted that there was not even a "special grant to give the children a treat at Christmas time. One would think they were back in the days of Dickens and his workhouses." He added, "At present in many cases, Residential Schools are not a credit to the Canadian public."[19]

In 1952, an inspector reported that the junior classroom had sixty-seven students,[20] which aligns with survivors' recollections of overcrowding. Ronald Wesley explained that there were about five grades per classroom during the time period the boys attended school at Pelican Lake.[21] Though one-room schooling was common in Ontario during this time period—and was even the norm—classroom sizes tended to max out at thirty students,[22] less than half of what was regularly reported at Pelican Lake. Consider, then, that even by the standards of the day, school inspectors were alarmed by what they observed there. Indian Agent Swartman, in a rare, indirect rebuke of DIA policy, wrote that "I have come to the conclusion that the children in our Residential Schools do not have sufficient recreation and opportunity to engage in sports and games. Actually they have not much time for such, owing to the endless chores and outside work."[23]

Kelly emphatically pointed out that overcrowding and limiting students to a half day of school are not acceptable by today's standards, nor were they accepted by the standards of the era. Administrators insisted that lack of classroom space was the reason that the half-day system continued to be practised.[24] Meanwhile, survivors' testimonies suggest that the school could not have functioned without them working for half the day. This was a contradiction that could be found at many, if not most, residential schools.[25] Lack of classroom space was a real issue, but also a convenient excuse for the limited academic curriculum at Pelican Lake.

Physical Education

Overall, informal games and recreational activities, rather than organized competitive sports, were the standard at Pelican Lake prior to the 1950s. According to the Anglican Church's records, from the school's beginning the lake was important to the school's recreation program, with swimming in the summer and skating or hockey in the winter.[26] In addition, calisthenics, sack races, and indoor play and recreation were also provided in designated spaces in the main school building.[27]

Like all aspects of student life, recreation and leisure periods at Pelican Lake were also rigidly segregated by gender, which in practice usually meant that the girls' physical activity received less attention and financial support than the boys'. Female residential school students were usually watched over very carefully in case they became too boisterous physically. More opportunities in general, and more opportunities for vigorous movements specifically, were provided for the boys. Kelly explained that to the best of his recollection, female students "used to walk down to the [railroad] track, which would be about a mile, and then back. I guess walks are good, but as we know exercise *today*, that did not happen." Seldom did female students have opportunities to engage in competitive sports, especially before the 1950s. This pattern was also seen in other schools within the residential school system. For instance, at Brandon Residential School, hockey (for boys only) was, in fact, the only sport referenced in its 1943–1944 yearbook.[28] However, the sporting picture was inconsistent, as the Brandon school fielded a girls' softball team in 1935, and there was a girls' baseball team at Assiniboia Residential School in the late 1950s. Indeed, other student accounts from Pelican Lake stated that both boys and girls played soccer and baseball. Boys played hockey on an outdoor rink, though their clothing was not warm enough for them to be outside for very long.[29] When local school administrators finally dedicated funds to make improvements to the inadequate playgrounds of the 1940s, they went to the boys' rather than the girls' playground.[30] The staff also organized hunting and fishing trips for the older boys, whose success was attributed by the committee to their "natural instincts and marksmanship."[31] Boys could often move about the residential school property with relative freedom. Kelly recalled that the male students had unsupervised time on Saturdays when they could hunt and fish on school grounds. Chris also remembers unstructured time swimming with other boys in Pelican Lake.

Even though the Anglican Church's administration in charge of Indian schools declared that "a thoroughly competent instructor" led physical training at Pelican Lake,[32] qualified instructors were hard to come by. When that reality is combined with the problem of continual staff turnover at the school, the offering of competent instruction was likely intermittent.

The lack of a safe and healthy recreation space at Pelican Lake, as was the case in most other residential schools across Canada, shows that the idealized vision for physical education that was promoted through official policy was far different from the realities of everyday school life. Though recalling events from decades before inevitably leads to some errors in recollection, it is evident from the first-hand accounts of Kelly, David, and Chris, as well as student recollections recorded elsewhere, that what was written in the "official" records was often at odds with what occurred "on the ground" at the school. This was illustrated when the DIA devised a policy of providing physical exercise in large and well-ventilated buildings during inclement weather;[33] however, one observer noted that the basement playroom of St. Peter's Residential School (in Cardston, Alberta) was a "grim, severe, [and] forebidding" space within a facility she called a "prison-reformatory."[34] At Pelican Lake during the same period, rainwater kept seeping into the basement, thus eliminating indoor activities for long stretches of time.[35] Principal Marshall had reported in 1930 that the water problem was so bad that the basement was almost like a swimming pool, which limited its use and made portions of the school particularly dangerous places to inhabit.[36] Astonishingly, by the time the Black Hawks enrolled at Pelican Lake almost twenty years later, repairs to the basement were still being called for.[37]

In 1945, Indian Agent Gifford Swartman complained that the "lack of recreational opportunities [was] very noticeable" at Pelican Lake Residential School and went on to note that "under proper supervision this would go a long way toward developing character and physique." Swartman was firm in the belief that Indigenous boys had a natural inclination towards sport, which could be used to build stronger bodies and better character.[38]

Despite a growing recognition of the need for these programs, sport and recreation opportunities were limited until 1947. The Missionary Society of the Church of England in Canada itself admitted that the Anglicans, who ran Pelican Lake, sometimes provided "scarcely any athletic activities" in their schools.[39] An official reported that although skate blades were available at the school, suitable boots to attach them to were not available.[40] He recommended the construction of a rink, but noted this would require additional resources, even though it was widely known that resources were hard to come by in the residential school system. The boys built their own playground as a "manual training project"[41] and had outsized responsibilities for creating their own recreation opportunities.

David explained that the male students were, at times, responsible for putting up and taking down their outdoor hockey rink: "They didn't supply sports. So, one guy asked if we could have some kind of game. . . . We had to cut the logs and then split [them] to build the [rink]."

"A Danger": Health and Illness

According to the administration, health was an important focus at the Pelican Lake school. The administration noted that close attention was paid to the children's health, which included lessons in sanitation, trained nurses at the school, access to additional nurses and doctors from Sioux Lookout, first aid and sanatorium bedrooms in the school's main building, and the daily provision of cod-liver oil.[42] Regardless of these claims, the poor health of students was a significant and recurring problem. In December 1937, a young boy became seriously ill; he passed away of tubercular meningitis early in 1938.[43] A report to Dr. Percy Moore, the superintendent of medical services at the DIA, explains the ways that the deplorable conditions endangered students: "The beds are so close that they touch at the sides. This is bad, especially where the children are as susceptible to respiratory disease and tuberculosis as are Indians. . . . Until something permanent can be done, the pupils should sleep head to foot alternately. I do not wish to be over-critical, but from the standpoint of public health the designation of a couple of three-bed rooms in Indian schools as preventoria is a travesty; if the entire residential school is not a preventorium what are we spending our money for?"[44]

In October of 1948, official G.R. Turner wrote a special memorandum regarding the poor conditions he noted when inspecting Pelican Lake. Turner described the buildings and premises as being in a "deplorable state of untidiness," and because livestock roamed freely there was "manure all over the place."[45] Turner was also particularly exasperated with the poor discipline among the students, as he saw it. At dinnertime, he reported, there were "stragglers" into meals, dining without first cleaning up, pupils wearing their caps in the dining hall, and general disorderly conduct. For Turner, the students' ill discipline and the lack of control over them were critical problems undermining the school's objectives.

Poor health, diet, and housing conditions were the norm. In the internal communications files that serve as a record of correspondence between, primarily, the three main parties involved in administering the school—the DIA, Anglican Church headquarters, and the school principal—such concerns were regularly discussed. Swartman reported that close behind a student death in March 1949, forty children were confined to bed because of a cold or flu epidemic. By suggesting that a nurse should be urgently dispatched to the school, Swartman inadvertently revealed that the institution lacked a resident qualified medical professional, without even a nurse on site.[46]

Later that year, the poor conditions at the school drew outside attention and condemnation. In September 1949, the MP from the

Kenora–Rainy River district, W.M. Benidickson, wrote that he and other visitors such as the Sioux Lookout mayor found the conditions of the school's restrooms "simply putrid." They were "astonished" that repairs were apparently going to be put off until the following fiscal year.[47] Diplomatically, he asked if funding could be found in the present year's budget so that the unhealthy conditions could be addressed immediately. This request came on the heels of a letter sent a few weeks prior by Swartman, who wrote that that toilets were in "very very bad condition."[48]

For once, things seemed to move along quickly at headquarters. The superintendent of the education division, Philip Phelan, reported that $5,000 had been allocated as a supplementary estimate for the 1949–50 fiscal year to address the school's plumbing problems. Furthermore, Phelan expected that he would be receiving bids from companies interested in doing the repairs within two or three weeks.[49] A local physician also wrote to the medical superintendent of Indian Health Services on 30 September to express his concerns about the school's plumbing: "The situation in general is unsanitary and a danger to the health of the children."[50] Despite their complaints, most of these letter writers also noted that the overall situation at the school seemed to be an *improvement* over conditions in recent years.

By December, though, an on-the-ground report indicated that no progress had been made in addressing the sanitation problems.[51] By February of the following year, 1950, Superintendent Cook of the Anglican Church reported that the toilets had been replaced, but other elements of the job remained unfinished.[52] A letter in May indicated that the repairs were still not completed.[53]

Only a few years prior, in 1946, the Board of Management for the General Synod of the Church of England's Indian Work Investigation Commission determined that major reforms would be required if the Church were to meet its objectives in educating Indigenous children. They concluded that if reorganization, increase in standards, improvement in conditions, and budgetary frugality could not be achieved, the operation of residential schools should be discontinued.[54] Pelican Lake was included on the list of schools to be scrapped.[55]

In 1951, Superintendent Cook conveyed his alarm to Phelan: "*In the interest of the health and comfort of the Indian children*" (emphasis in original), conditions at the school, such as ongoing problems with sewage disposal, must be addressed immediately.[56] Years had now elapsed since problems with the plumbing had been identified. Recall, also, that manure was said to be prolific on the school grounds. In 1953, the school was reported to be under "quarantine" due to an unspecified illness, which was evidently serious, as children were transported by boat to the closest hospital.[57]

Such treatment had only recently become available, as survivors have confirmed that proper medical facilities were not provided for students until the opening of the hospital in Sioux Lookout in 1949. Even then, such care was intermittent and could be refused without explanation. Giving testimony on the institution's earlier years, one student, Esther Faries, could not remember ever seeing an inspector from the DIA or a doctor at the school over the seven years she spent at Pelican Lake. Even though there was a nurse on duty, "many children died."[58] Note the direct contrast between her experience and the statements about the importance of students' health above. The National Centre for Truth and Reconciliation's Memorial Register lists more than twenty students who died at or went missing from Pelican Lake Residential School.[59] Given the recent revelations about the discovery of unmarked graves at former residential school sites across the country, this number is likely an undercount.

Chris's testimony for the Truth and Reconciliation Commission captures the disregard for student health at the institution: "Even though a lot of times once somebody caught something. . . it spread in the whole school like wildfire, and . . . more or less, we had to live out whatever it is that we caught, whether it's measles, mumps, sores, bedbugs, all that kind of stuff, we just had to live with it."[60] Chris suffered jaundice from an unknown cause. Kelly recalled his finger having been broken by the principal and never receiving proper medical care for it. It causes him pain and restricts movement to this day, some seventy years after the injury.

Despite the stated intent in 1946 to close substandard schools, including Pelican Lake, nothing changed. The DIA's Educational Survey Officer pointed out in 1951 that medical officials had recently criticized the food provided to students at the school and concluded that "an increase in expenditure on food so as to come up to the standard recommended seems necessary in order to avoid undernutrition, malnutrition and monotony."[61] Concerns about the students' diet had been discussed since at least 1946. That year, a dietary survey of nine residential schools concluded that they were all meeting basic standards, if barely—except Pelican Lake.[62] Therefore, while a select few were taken on the no-expense-spared hockey tour of Southern Ontario, the school did not have the financial resources to adequately feed its students.

Order and Discipline

Without question, the financial policies of the DIA contributed to the poor state of Pelican Lake. It could not simply be attributed to the deficient school culture and failed leadership of its principals. However, hope reigned that a personnel change would improve matters. By June of 1949, the school principal had been replaced with Reverend Wilson, who they hoped would usher in a new era of leadership, order, and pupil discipline.

Chris remembers Wilson as a cruel taskmaster with an apparent hostility towards even the most minor expressions of the students' cultures. Wilson struck Chris from behind on the back of the head and dragged him into his office when he overheard Chris greeting his friend's family members in Ojibwemowin upon their arrival to fetch their son from the institution. Kelly stated that Wilson was so cruel that the very sight of him caused Kelly to shake with fear. Worse still, for unknown reasons Principal Wilson selected Kelly to be a kind of personal servant, solely responsible for keeping dry wood constantly stocked on the school verandah. Kelly explained how on winter mornings he had to ensure that instead of wet, frozen logs, Wilson had dry kindling to start his stove and keep the school warm: "And whenever I didn't fulfill those tasks, he found ways to strap me or something, like—to teach me a lesson that I've got to do what I'm told."

Figure 5. From Christmas 1946, Chris Cromarty is shown in this photo. He is seated to the right of the tinselled pole with his hand near his face. P7538-1038. From the Anglican Church of Canada's MSCC fonds. Reproduced with permission.

Despite occasional dire proclamations from inspectors, visitors, or the school employees of Pelican Lake themselves, the sad state of affairs was stubbornly resistant to change. Survivor testimonies across the residential school system indicate that this type of casual cruelty was common; yet, calls for reform system-wide and at Pelican Lake went unanswered. Many students who passed through the system experienced abuse under the guise of discipline: "schools 'disciplined' students for (minor) infractions or perceived misconduct with severe beatings, starvation, isolation and enforced labour."[63]

School administrators, unsurprisingly, used discipline and order as the bedrock of school routine. It is difficult to adequately capture just how different Kelly's life became after being forced to leave home and enroll at Pelican Lake: "Things changed drastically from what I was used to living in Whitefish Bay, running through the woods, wind blowing through your hair, out swimming with the other children. We were in this regimented setup [at the school]."

Prayers and religious education were also regular features of school life, and short chapel services were held twice daily, at 8 a.m. and 7 p.m. for pupils and staff.[64] For Chris, the religious emphasis of their weekly routines, such as having to attend church or chapel services three times on Sunday, was particularly stifling.

Happy moments were rare at Pelican Lake. Holidays and other special occasions broke the monotony and also offered something else in short supply—new or special foods. Chris fondly remembers an annual Victoria Day picnic with homemade ice cream and hot dogs. When he examined Figure 5, where he can be seen to the right of the tinselled pole with his arm near his face, the photograph was not familiar to him. He knew, though, that it had to have been Christmas because "we never decorated anything except for special days." Chris also remembers these two occasions as the only times throughout the year that he got to see his sisters; since they were different ages, they did not have classes together as some other students might. When Kelly saw this photograph, he recognized Chris right away. He noticed that they are wearing their suits at dinner and that meant it had to have been a special occasion. (Their usual clothing was often insufficient for the weather or the activity at hand; upon seeing Figure 6, Kelly remarked, "See, look how poorly we were dressed, and we were still playing outdoors. But the kids were tough.") In another student's account of attending Pelican Lake sometime in the 1930s to early 1940s, she fondly recalled a Christmas dinner that boasted roast beef, mashed potatoes, turnips, and dessert. The children received gifts and they were permitted to talk "Indian" to each other. Her father came to the school to visit her and her siblings. She asked herself, "Why was it only at Christmas that we were shown kindness and respect, and not all year long?"[65]

Figure 6. Boys playing outdoors in the winter at Pelican Lake Residential School, c. 1950. Reproduced with permission from Shingwauk Residential Schools Centre (Algoma University). From an album of photographs that belonged to former Pelican Lake staff member Joyce Clinton.

CHAPTER 5

HOCKEY WILL MAKE THINGS BETTER

The Unlikely Champions: The Black Hawks, 1948–1951

Until the fall of 1948, the only facility for skating and hockey at the school had been a small rink cleared on Pelican Lake. By October of 1948, interest in building a rink grew, and the Anglican administration for Indian schools was asked to approve the use of lumber from a dismantled building for the new outdoor facility.[1] Soon the rink was under construction.[2] Indian Agent Gifford Swartman was likely the key initiator behind the rink's development, as the school principal and the Anglican administration for Indian schools claimed to be unaware of the cost, even though Swartman had previously asked them for financial support.[3] The rink was located on the playing field behind the school, and it thus had to be constructed every fall and dismantled every spring to allow for use of the playing field during the warmer months.[4] David recalls that the work to put up and dismantle the rink sometimes fell to the boys, even though the superintendent stated to his superior that employees completed this work.[5]

With a new and improved skating facility in hand, Swartman approached Art Schade, a local businessman from Sioux Lookout, to gauge his interest in helping Swartman form a pupil hockey team.[6] Schade enthusiastically agreed and around Christmas of 1948 the club and its administrative structure was established with Schade as president, Wickenden, school principal, as honourary president, Swartman as secretary, and Pete Seymour as the coach. Seymour, who was an Indigenous school staff member, was described as a "good carpenter and sports promoter" who spent a lot of time with the boys and was a good influence on them.[7] Survivors recall Seymour as a "part Native" or "Métis/half-breed" ally who invited the male students to listen to *Hockey Night in Canada* on the radio in his living quarters and who secretly spoke Ojibwemowin with them. He had graduated from St. Mary's Indian Residential School some years before and brought his knowledge and enthusiasm for hockey to Pelican Lake. His efforts quickly paid off. Four others rounded out the executive committee.[8] Swartman was the key figure in forming the Pelican Lake team, but the Black Hawks were the result of a collective effort that included support from the DIA, the Anglican Church's Indian school administrative body, and the school principal, as well as donations and support from Sioux Lookout citizens.[9]

Similar to other minor hockey teams throughout the nation at the time, the team's namesake and insignia were adopted from a professional hockey team: in this instance, the Chicago Black Hawks. Kelly assumes that it was the "Indian connotation" that led the administration to select the Black Hawks as the team's name and logo, though he does not recall that he or other students had any say in the name's selection. Although it is difficult to know how many other residential school hockey teams existed during the tenure of the residential school system, the Sioux Lookout Black Hawks were not the only Black Hawks in the system: Brandon Residential School's hockey team was also called the Black Hawks,[10] and many other residential schools—especially in the prairies—boasted champion school hockey teams.

None of the boys trying out for the team had ever skated before, making the establishment of the hockey team an impressive feat. Soon the Black Hawks were entered as a bantam-aged team into the Sioux

Lookout and District Hockey League. Tryouts for the Black Hawks team began on the new school rink in December of 1948. None of the boys had skates or sticks, so both were supplied by donations from local citizens as well as through a grant from the DIA. Within a few days, the coaches reported that a dozen boys could skate the length of the ice without falling.[11] Their first game was scheduled for the Sioux Lookout Memorial Arena in the first week of January 1949. Although the Black Hawks did not stand out as a team in their first competitive year, they improved steadily through the season, such that in the following year, they were a different calibre team. They started their second year with a pre-season exhibition game against an older midget team from Sioux Lookout, and a 3–1 Black Hawks win was a promising sign.[12]

In the 1949–1950 season, the Black Hawks gave up only fourteen goals in thirteen games and lost only one game in both the regular and post-season on their way to winning the Sioux Lookout and District Championship.[13] This was a far cry from struggling to skate the length of the ice without falling just one season ago. The Black Hawks were a revelation. In March of 1950, the *Indian School Bulletin* reproduced an article originally written in the Sioux Lookout newspaper, the *Daily Bulletin*, which spoke of the success and style of play the Black Hawks brought to the district:

> Monday night at the local arena the Indian Residential School Black Hawks played a brand of hockey never before seen by local fans so far this season. The Hawks thoroughly shellacked an over-sized Hudson team by a 6–1 score. The arena was really packed at last night's encounter and there was never a dull moment during the fast, hard-hitting game put on by both clubs. The last time these two teams met the Hawks were edged out by Hudson 3–2, but there was no doubt in anyone's mind as to who played a superior brand of hockey last night and the Hawks really deserve credit for their fine win.[14]

As Sioux Lookout champions, the Black Hawks then travelled to Geraldton, Ontario to play the highly rated Geraldton bantam team for the Thunder Bay District Championship.[15] The Black Hawks beat Geraldton in three straight games.

The boys were also making a name for themselves off the ice. The manager of the hotel the boys stayed at in Geraldton let them know that they would be welcome back anytime, as he noted, "it was the first hockey team which had ever behaved properly!"[16] Also, in the 1949–1950 season the Black Hawks travelled to Kenora to play in their first all-Indian residential school tournament that included Fort Francis, Cecilia Jeffrey, and McIntosh schools. News of the Indigenous hockey phenoms reached DIA headquarters in Ottawa, causing the Superintendent of Education to remark approvingly, "I have heard a great deal about the hockey team at Sioux Lookout and imagine the game on Saturday night with McIntosh should be a Red Letter Day in the lives of the pupils from both schools who will be playing."[17]

In the summer of 1950, Eisenhardt, the DIA's new superintendent of physical education and recreation, travelled from Ottawa to the Sioux Lookout Rotary Club to award the prizes for the local hockey league. He stood upon the stage and, one by one, the Black Hawks filed past and received a wooden trophy, whereupon each boy turned towards the audience and said, "thank you." From conversations with locals at the event, Eisenhardt learned that citizens who had a rather low opinion of Indigenous Peoples began to change their minds because of teams such as the Black Hawks, who, when given a chance, demonstrated that they were able to achieve something great.[18]

At Pelican Lake, general enthusiasm for hockey was catching on, though not all students had equal access to their new favourite pastime. Instructors encouraged "any interested student" to take up the sport and develop as a player, although this probably excluded female students.[19] According to the superintendent, by the winter of 1950, games of hockey for the boys, and skating for the boys and girls, were at the heart of the physical education program at the school.[20] Though Cook noted that all students used the rink "whenever possible,"[21] implying that girls also used the facility, Chris and Kelly could not recall girls ever having access to skates—a scarce resource.

In April 1951, the Department of Citizenship and Immigration, which the DIA fell into during this period, and the Department of Health and Welfare co-sponsored a friendly boys' competition between the bantam-aged Black Hawks and the top playground teams in Ottawa and Toronto. The primary purpose of the trip was ostensibly to reward the Black Hawks for their "ability, behavior and sportsmanship" on the ice.[22] A second reason called attention to the nationalistic purposes of sport; the government hoped "to encourage hockey among Canada's Indians."[23] Further to these objectives were the intangible benefits that the students would supposedly accrue from this excursion. As one of their coaches for the trip south, Bruce McCully, explained to the *Ottawa Journal*, "These three days in Ottawa will be worth three years' schooling for the boys."[24] The trip was simultaneously an educational project to introduce the youth to the nation's cultural centre, which included, among other things, tours of the National Archives, National Museum, and Parliament Buildings in Ottawa, and a media-generated spectacle to promote the integration of Indigenous students into the public-school system. In the eyes of the federal government, assimilation was the goal of the entire residential schooling endeavour. The tour, therefore, also encouraged assimilation by bringing Indigenous and non-Indigenous youth together in friendly, competitive play. In 1947, the DIA had written that sports and recreation "provide the best opportunities for the Indian child to experience accepted social practices and to associate with the white child on a common ground."[25] Figures 7 and 8 visually demonstrate the coming together of Indigenous boys and white boys in the tour, framed reassuringly by smiling representatives from the upper echelons of the white Canadian socio-political class.

The small, remote, and close-knit First Nations communities in Northern Ontario, and the underfunded, struggling, and problem-ridden residential school that their children went to, were worlds apart from an all-expenses-paid tour of the modern, metropolitan, and bustling cities of Toronto and Ottawa. Not a single Black Hawks

Figure 7. Black Hawks player Ernest Wesley faces off against a player from the Ottawa team during the April 1951 tour. Two ex-NHL players and current members of Parliament who refereed one of the Black Hawks' games, Wilfred "Bucko" McDonald (*right*) and Lionel Conacher (*left*), look on (in white shirts). The man in the dark suit with glasses is Paul Martin Sr. Taken by NFB photographer Gar Lunney. AFC 451-S5-F14, 56972, 6-5.2-33, 1950–1951. From Archives and Special Collections, Western Libraries, Western University. Used with permission.

Figure 8. Black Hawks player Albert Carpenter shakes the hand of an opposing player from the local Ottawa league during the April 1951 tour. Taken by NFB photographer Gar Lunney. AFC 451-S5-F14, 56960, 6-5.2-27, 1950–1951. From Archives and Special Collections, Western Libraries, Western University. Used with permission.

Figure 9. Black Hawks Albert Carpenter (*left*) and Ernest Wesley (*right*) pose with former NHL players and then members of Parliament Wilfred "Bucko" McDonald (*left*) and Lionel Conacher (*right*) during one of the Ottawa games on the April 1951 tour. Taken by NFB photographer Gar Lunney. AFC 451-S5-F14, 56974, 6-5.2-33, 1950–1951. From Archives and Special Collections, Western Libraries, Western University. Used with permission.

player could have ever dreamed his education would include something as unlikely as this hockey excursion. Travelling with the team were key personnel from the Black Hawks committee, including Wilson, Swartman, Schade, and the mayor of Sioux Lookout and club president, William Fuller; McCully served as coach.[26] The tour consisted of three games, one game each against the East Browns and Combines of Ottawa and one game against Shopsy's of Toronto. The transition from a semi-permanent rink constructed from salvaged lumber and located in the woods of Northern Ontario to Ottawa's Auditorium and Toronto's Maple Leaf Gardens shows how far the boys had come. Two former professional hockey players and current members of Parliament, Wilfred "Bucko" McDonald and Lionel Conacher, refereed the East

Figure 10. The Black Hawks in action (shown here in a game in Ottawa, Ontario, during their April 1951 tour). In the centre right, wearing the striped Black Hawks jersey (#12), is Jerry Ross. The other Black Hawk visible on the right side of the image is Eddie Mandamin. Taken by NFB photographer Gar Lunney. AFC 451-S5-F14, 56969, 6-5.2-37, 1950–1951. From Archives and Special Collections, Western Libraries, Western University. Used with permission.

Browns game.[27] See Figure 9 for a photograph of these men in a paternalistic pose with two of the Black Hawks, Albert Carpenter and Ernest Wesley. The Black Hawks beat the East Browns and then later lost to the Combines.

Media coverage of the Ottawa games reached as far as the prairies, where H.L. Jones of the *Saskatoon Star-Phoenix* highlighted the gentlemanly conduct of the Black Hawks, writing, "there was no scalping, rough-house or angry words. Just clean play, goodwill all around and smiles, especially Indian smiles."[28] Other newspaper coverage of the Black Hawks focused on their courteous behaviour, even in victory: "The Black Hawks went about their chores in a business-like manner and even if they did pin defeat on the Browns they made it painless by

Figure 11. Another action shot of the Black Hawks during one of their Ottawa matches on their April 1951 tour. In the centre wearing a striped jersey (#12) is Black Hawks player Jerry Ross. To his right, seen in profile, is likely Black Hawks player Frank Wesley. Further right, with his stick outstretched, is Black Hawk Eddie Mandamin. Taken by NFB photographer Gar Lunney. AFC 451-S5-F14, 56970, 6-5.2-37, 1950–1951. From Archives and Special Collections, Western Libraries, Western University. Used with permission.

presenting their opponents with lacrosse sticks as a token of friendship between the second and third periods."[29] For two photographs of the Ottawa games featuring on-ice action with Black Hawks Jerry Ross, Eddie Mandamin, and Frank Wesley, see Figures 10 and 11.

The *Ottawa Evening Citizen* commented on the spectator enjoyment provided by the Black Hawks' style of play, as "hockey fans who passed up the show missed a fast, clean match that thrilled the spectators from start to finish."[30] Jones, from the *Star-Phoenix*, pointed out the most expressive example of their sportsmanlike conduct, when "Walter Kakepetum, scored two goals, but got the night's only penalty as Bucko sent him off for hooking."[31] The *Ottawa Citizen* added that Kakepetum "was so bewildered that he couldn't find the sin-bin. Ironically enough, who should lead him to it but Bucko McDonald and Lionel Conacher."[32] The irony alluded to was the reversal of roles, as the typically clean and sportsmanlike Black Hawks player was led to the penalty box by former professional players who were known for their rough play.

From the Auditorium the Black Hawks travelled to the Maple Leaf Gardens, where they took on and lost to the local Shopsy's team. Media coverage in Toronto also pointed to the contrast between the Black Hawks' style of play and that of competitive Canadian hockey teams. The *Telegram* was appreciative of the way in which Shopsy's played without their normal aggressive edge, commenting that the team was not "playing as rough as they, or any local minor club can. Normally an aggressive outfit, they played this one clean on the sportsmanlike instruction of Coach Oscar Brooks and Manager Jack Humphreys. Even at that they absorbed all six penalties."[33] Other press coverage reported that even when the Black Hawks were losing "they never lost even part of their determination. Though four goals behind in the period's dying moments, they were still playing with everything at their command. Still, they weren't rough. In fact, they were given no penalties, compared to five issued to the Toronto team."[34] From a publicity point of view, the significant Black Hawks media coverage clearly paid dividends for the Anglican church and the DIA. The press coverage of their sportsmanlike play provided public validation of the church's and the DIA's efforts to use sport to develop good character among residential school students. One observer from the Presbyterian Church wrote of seeing the Black Hawks play in Toronto: "It was heart warming to hear the applause when they got the puck and appeared as though they were going to get away with it. Of course, most of the people who were there were from the various Anglican Churches throughout the city. I think it will do much to create a greater interest in the Indian work."[35]

The Black Hawks' itinerary was full of educational activities that included meetings with dignitaries to mark the occasion. Upon arriving in Ottawa, the Black Hawks were greeted by the mayor before heading to the parliament buildings.[36] The Kenora Member of Parliament led the boys on a guided tour of the House of Commons before they completed their first day with a swim at their hotel, the ritzy Chateau Laurier.

The Black Hawks went on another guided tour on the following day, this time to two civic icons, the National Museum and the National Archives. Then, prior to the East Browns game, Governor General Alexander and a veritable who's who of the senior leadership of the DIA came out to greet the boys. The list included the Superintendent of the DIA, Walter Harris; Minister of National Health and Welfare, Paul Martin; Deputy Minister of Citizenship and Immigration, Laval Fortier; Director of the DIA, D.M. Mackay; Director of Indian Health Services, Dr. Percy Moore; and Superintendent of Indian Education, Philip Phelan.[37] In Toronto, the Black Hawks continued their sightseeing adventures, including a trip to Queen's Park to meet the Premier of Ontario, Leslie Frost, an old friend of Swartman's.

As with the other dignitaries, Frost enjoyed publicity snapshots with the boys, which were arranged both on and off the ice.[38] Additionally, the Black Hawks publicity campaign included appearances on local radio shows.[39] From a competitive standpoint, two losses and one win did not amount to a particularly successful tour. Yet what happened off the ice was, for the tour organizers, an equally if not more important aspect. Black Hawks manager Schade stated that from an educational perspective the tour was "well worth" the cost.[40] The education referred to was the key motivation behind the tour, and it did not involve reading, math, or science. Rather, it was an essential lesson in citizenship.[41]

When the tour was over, the boys returned to their daily routine at school, capping off their 1950–1951 season with a game in Fort William, where they played and lost two exhibition games.[42] The emerging Montreal Canadiens superstar Maurice "Rocket" Richard signed autographs and featured in a photo opportunity with the boys after refereeing a game. The young boys had become a well-known team and a compelling story in many rinks and households throughout the province, and the role of the Black Hawks, and hockey generally, had also become an important part of life back at Pelican Lake school.

Some of the staff—for example, the Indigenous supervisor Pete Seymour, who also served as their hockey coach at school (but was not part of the 1951 Southern Ontario tour)—and volunteers, such as local businessman Art Schade and bakery owner Oreste Tintinalli ("a good guy," according to Kelly), who shuttled the boys to games in his bread van, were good-hearted and motivated to help disadvantaged youth achieve athletic success. Kelly remembers, with fondness, that they took a keen interest in the boys and encouraged them. Kelly also took pains to point to others who were gentle, positive influences on the boys, and does not want their kindnesses to be forgotten. Recently, he told Alexandra about a former supervisor who came to visit the Black Hawks in their dressing room at the Ottawa rink bearing a large fruit basket. Kelly remembers him as a sympathetic individual who was of a different character than many of the other adults at the school. Sponsors were also generous financially. Chris fondly recalls being treated to ice cream and pie after every game—surely no small expense, with the bill likely being footed by Schade, as the school administrators would not have been permitted such expenses.

Yet telling the "whole story" of the Sioux Lookout Black Hawks means understanding that school staff and administrators used hockey for other, less generous, purposes—like maintaining student discipline and discouraging runaways. Sport was said to have raised the morale of the school as well as brought its pupils under tighter control.[43] Although hockey was only for the boys, and the Black Hawks were a group of only twelve players, the impact of hockey and the rink on school spirit was significant. The benefits of hockey were considered to be a school-wide effect by the regional supervisor of the DIA in 1951.[44] Indian Agent Swartman noted another example of the importance of the positive impact of hockey on student discipline. In July of 1951, he was clear in his opinion that hockey was a means for enhancing student compliance, arguing, "a rink at this school is almost as essential as a classroom because there had been no truancy since the rink has been in operation."[45]

That hockey and other forms of recreation had a positive impact on student conduct was noticed across the residential school system. At Brandon Residential School, a regional inspector investigating runaways and other issues noted that a male student complained of having no opportunity for play and was sad about the loss of hockey and baseball. Thirteen students had run away during the previous school year, 1950–51.[46] In a follow-up assessment some six years later, the regional supervisor identified a recreational director as one of the school's "greatest needs."[47] The school's temporary principal agreed, pointing out that the school had neither a playground nor a gymnasium. He drove his point home by linking play activities to the school's mission: "GOOD SPORTSMANSHIP IS A NECESSARY PART OF CHRISTIAN LIVING" (emphasis in original).[48] In contrast, reflecting on the improvements that the school's new principal had achieved a year later, the assistant regional supervisor pointed out the school's "excellent skating rink of regulation size and well maintained and equipped."[49] The rink, along with road repairs, new buildings, good food, a new approach to discipline, and high-quality staff, had resulted in happier students and no runaways over the previous five months.[50]

Though the boys tried to obey the rules that governed their lives at Pelican Lake in order to be able to engage in the activities that brought them happiness and relief, the principal seemed determined to emphasize that no aspect of the students' lives was beyond his control. Kelly recalls being mercilessly strapped after being caught trying to retrieve his skates in the hallway in front of the principal's office, where the team had left their bags after returning to school late the previous evening. Even though Kelly had dutifully completed his chores that Saturday before attempting to play hockey, it seemed that the rules had changed. Kelly explained: "I was going to grab my skates and go out on the rink and skate and Wilson [the principal] caught me—I guess he heard the noise [as] I was unzippering my bag to get at my skates: 'Who's out there?' I said, 'I'm getting my hockey equipment.' And [he said], 'Who told you to do that?' I said, 'Nobody,' and he said, 'You don't do anything unless you're told.' And, you know, for that he gave me a good strapping because I didn't toe the line; I didn't follow the instructions."

The boys at Pelican Lake may have only learned part of the classroom curriculum, but they did learn another cruel lesson at school: what was given could be easily taken away, and the stakes were even higher when it came to the limited parts of institutional life that brought the boys pleasure. Chris recalls the principal burning a student's skates as a punishment, an action that had clear—and likely crushing—consequences for the boy in question, as having his own pair of skates would have been considered a privilege. Chris remembered that it was quite some time before he was given his own pair, though second-hand and the wrong size. The skate-burning punishment would have had obvious symbolism as well. The school administrators were aware of the happiness that skating and playing hockey brought the boys: "That the rink served as a means to increase student morale, happiness, and compliance was well-understood."[51] By taking the skates away in such a public and dramatic manner, the principal demonstrated control over the one area of life at the institution that brought the players fleeting moments of happiness, mastery, and escape from the drudgery of their everyday lives. Chris explains: "They took the skates away and put them in the fire, just to punish [the student] or punish us or show us as an example what can happen."

Not surprisingly, getting to participate in hockey ultimately failed to deter student resistance. In March of 1953, administrators reported an "epidemic" of truancy that had been in full swing since the beginning of that year—which meant that prime skating and hockey season had failed to keep runaways at bay.[52] In 1961, a decade after the Black Hawks tour, officials again reported a "spate of runaways" from the institution. This time, Cook, the Anglican Church superintendent, directly linked students fleeing the school with insufficient sport and recreational opportunities and suggested that the situation might improve when the ice rink froze over for the season.[53] Although the rink allowed some students an outlet for part of the year, complaints about a lack of recreational space, play equipment, and sports equipment persisted until the 1960s when budget allocations improved,[54] though it was not until 1962 that students had a gymnasium.[55] Former Pelican Lake student Ronald Wesley said in his 1972 CBC interview with Johnny Yesno and Kelly Bull that the school's runaway problem "should be an example of how much these Indian kids [who] were taken to these schools—how much they hated it. I mean, you never hear of boys running away from Upper Canada College [an Ontario elite preparatory school]."[56] In conversation with Alexandra, Kelly stated an important truth:

> **Kelly:** The government and church recognized there was a problem. Why were kids running away?

The Symbolism of Indigenous Boys Playing "Canada's Game"

Images of the young boys from a rural residential school playing Canada's great game against white urban-based teams provided an ideal canvas on which to project colonial narratives about sport, specifically hockey, and integration.[57] The media often relied on stereotypes about an imagined "uncivilized" past to describe the Black Hawks, while at the same time contrasting that image with a mythical "civilizing" present. It was a narrative that suggested hockey, when monitored and controlled by the proper authorities, could be a more effective tool for integration than schooling—at least for Indigenous youth. Hockey was more than just a fun pastime.

At the same time, the administrators at Pelican Lake benefitted from a system-wide effort to expand and develop physical education. Hockey's success was a central feature in the perceived administrative successes of the entire school. The DIA and the Anglican Church intended the lessons of what it meant to be a good athlete to be translated into what it meant to be a good person *off* the ice as well. Journalists made constant reference to the Black Hawks' clean play, humility in victory, and never-say-die competitive spirit. These noble qualities were best captured in the media coverage through the symbolism of Walter Kakepetum's bewildered and failed search for the penalty box.

Furthermore, the DIA intended the off-ice activities, such as experiencing the lifestyle of capital cities, the national institutions of cultural and civic importance, and the flurry of meetings with dignitaries, to have lasting value. The education intended by the DIA rationalized the progress of modern urban life, the developments of civilization, and the opportunities and way of life that Canadian society offered. The DIA presented this perspective to the Black Hawks in a lavish and carefully constructed tour offered exclusively for the boys, and the print and radio media retold this story to the public.

Indeed, the pleasant, well-behaved, and polite boys impressed those whom they encountered on this tour as well as on their various other hockey trips. The ethical reputation and style of play of the Black Hawks was, when compared to professional and even minor competitive Canadian hockey, a nostalgic expression of values that many hockey fans and coaches believed ought to be followed. Journalists used this romanticized view of hockey, one that aligned with the clean, fast, and talented positional play of the Black Hawks, as a statement of desired values that were inconsistent with the increasingly physical, aggressive, and cynical nature of competitive hockey.

Yet, no matter how well the Black Hawks played, or however much they played according to prevailing standards of "gentlemanly" conduct, they could not escape the racial undertones that permeated the newspaper reports. Their potential for integration was thus always mediated by race-based views of such potential.

Public performances—including sports—of colonized peoples were a relatively common occurrence throughout the British Empire and often went hand-in-glove with imperial goals. Sport and leisure clubs, media, and governments were all implicated in these displays, which often reinforced the power imbalance between settlers and colonial subjects. An 1868 tour of Aboriginal cricketers in England, during which players visiting from Australia also engaged in spear-throwing demonstrations, illustrates how sport can be a "venue of racialized public performance."[58] Sherwood, Osmond, and Phillips analyze the portrayal of rugby league games in the Queensland, Australia, media between Aboriginal residents from local settlements and white opponents from the 1920s to the 1950s. They note that government and settlement officials clearly understood how public sporting events could serve to convince the public that Aboriginal people were undergoing much-needed socio-cultural transformations. Aboriginal and non-Aboriginal people were kept quite separate during this period, and rugby—with its distinct ties to Australian national identity—was a rare chance for white Australians "to witness, or read, about the 'advancement' of Aboriginal people and contemplate their inclusion in the national future."[59] Indigenous youth engaged in sport, both witnessed "live" and in professional photographs distributed through the press, would have similarly had a visual impact on Canadian audiences.

It is worth re-emphasizing that hockey had special significance for the Canadian public, the desired tour audience. As it is now, hockey then was seen to represent Canadian identity itself. Hockey is said almost mythically to have sprung from the rugged Northern landscape that Euro-Canadians encountered when settling the lands that we now call Canada.[60] Though the origins of hockey are actually debated, settlers are often presented as its inventors and the game seen as a site of "authentic" belonging for white Canadians. In turn, the game, "naturally and uniquely Canadian," has been idealized as an activity free from the inequalities present in broader society.[61] It has also been idealized as a "force of social cohesion."[62]

Kelly had some difficulty making sense of the idea that the public might think that residential school was tolerable because they got to play hockey. He said, "I don't know what it means. Because we played hockey—is [that] being interpreted as us accepting the school?" Alexandra had to explain that, yes, some Canadians did think that residential schools were "not that bad" because, the thinking goes, at least the students got to play sports. Somewhat confused, he asked for further clarification: "I don't get you . . . unless the interpretation is, 'Consider yourself lucky you played hockey'?" This misconception occurred throughout the course of this project. One museum employee remarked to Alexandra that she was happy to hear a "positive story about a residential school." The Black Hawks tour might have drawn public attention away from the overall deprivation of life at Pelican Lake outside of hockey. However, those who lived through it cannot forget the absence of educational opportunities, the forced labour, and the lack of care and resources for students that characterized their lives at the school.

CHAPTER 6

A MEANS OF ESCAPE

Kelly came into a collection of photographs, news clippings, and handwritten notes about the Black Hawks years ago when a contact at the DIA saved these items and a scrapbook from being thrown out. This scrapbook is the one referenced in the Preface. We assume that the person who assembled the scrapbook was Gifford Swartman's secretary, as she was the one who eventually saved the scrapbook from the junkyard and got it to Kelly. Kelly also remembers her as an engaged fan of the Black Hawks. In its pages, she recorded each goal, assist, and penalty, as well as extra details on occasion, such as for a game on 27 January 1950: "1st period. (Score 1–0). Hudson made first goal. Black Hawks a little discouraged but still determined." Figure 12 shows the cover of the scrapbook.

The enthusiasm conveyed within the scrapbook's pages mirrors the exhilaration that the Black Hawks themselves felt out on the ice.

> **Alexandra**: You talked about how it was a good feeling to be out there in the woods [when you had free time at residential school]. You felt like some of the pressure was off. Did you feel that same way playing hockey?
>
> **Kelly:** Well, the challenge was there. I guess that was the big thing. How fast you skated and how hard your shot was.

Figure 12. Cover page of the Black Hawks scrapbook, found in Kelly's collection, for the 1949–1950 season. From the personal collection of Kelly Bull. Used with permission.

> I think things picked up when we were introduced to that [former] National Hockey League player, Jack MacDonald.[1] He really taught us a lot of small things. How to take a man out. Where to position. Anticipation.

It is easy to imagine his and his peers' excitement from the very first night they were introduced to hockey. Pete Seymour, the boys' supervisor and hockey coach, invited them into his quarters to listen to *Hockey Night in Canada* on the radio: "We were all gathered around. . . . We would pick up names [from the hockey broadcast] and then the next morning when we were out playing hockey, we would pretend we were that guy," said Kelly.

Referencing Figure 13, Kelly commented on the boys' ingenuity:

> **Kelly:** This is how we would play . . . You see, this is how we got started, eh. We would be playing shinny out in the cleared-out area. These sticks were not store bought. We made those ourselves.
>
> **Alexandra:** How did you learn how to make them?
>
> **Kelly**: We would . . . Mr. McCully's shop had all kinds of tools, and we would—well, it came in two pieces. There was the straight piece, and then this little piece is what we would make inside the shop. You know, we'd cut it and then screw it on or nail it on, whatever.

Some seventy years later, Chris still remembered who was playing that night as he listened to the radio in Seymour's room: the Maple Leafs against the New York Rangers. Looking at Figure 13, even though he is not in the photograph, seemed to transport Chris back to those days: "Once we begun to have skates, everybody on the boys' side just became fanatics for hockey. Totally. We weren't supposed to wake up until seven o'clock in the morning. We were sneaking down at four in the morning. Just to skate on the rink and play hockey."

When Chris and Alexandra picked up their discussion the following day, he was keen to impress upon her the importance of hockey for providing a kind of release valve for the stress, anger, and sadness of having to live at Pelican Lake Residential School. They played any way and any time they could, employing a rubber ball as a makeshift puck and brooms as hockey sticks to play in the field in the off-season months. "It took us away from the drudgery" of the everyday routine. When Chris was back home for the summer, he taught his brothers to play. And when Alexandra asked him if hockey had taken on a special meaning given how isolated he was and how difficult life was at the school, he was one step ahead of her: "I've thought a lot about it since I saw you yesterday because I knew you were going to ask that question, and once we got wind of it, once we were able to get skates, we became fanatics for hockey. Everything we did. But what it did

Figure 13. Image of boys playing hockey in the Pelican Lake Indian Residential School's yard in the 1940s. Reproduced with permission from Shingwauk Residential Schools Centre (Algoma University).

was once we found out there was professional hockey through the radio, there was something beyond the residential school. So, your dreams began."

There is no question that Chris loved playing hockey at Pelican Lake. But for him, perhaps more than the others, the game was also symbolic of a life beyond the residential school doors. Though he may not have put it this way himself, hockey helped Chris see a future in the wider world after residential school. He encountered some of the world beyond Pelican Lake's boundaries when he and the team headed to Thunder Bay (then Fort William-Port Arthur) for a tournament called the Rendezvous. The team got to stay at the Prince Arthur, at the time a high-end CN hotel, in Port Arthur (see Figure 14 for a photograph from the time period and Figure 15 for an image of the Black Hawks with Maurice "Rocket" Richard in Thunder Bay). Chris recalled what a shock city life was to him. It was his first time staying in a hotel—a serious upgrade from the crowded and dingy living quarters at the residential school. The experience was "a pleasure." He expanded: "I had never even been in a town larger than Sioux Lookout. . . . I'd never seen a lot of stuff I saw for the first time. . . . surrounded by stores, streets . . . [The food at the hotel] was the best we ever had. . . . Namely, it was different."

Arguably, Kelly was the player for whom the sporting experiences at the school would have the most impact over the course of the rest of his life. As a physical and emotional outlet, sports had been his lifesaver at Pelican Lake. Kelly spent most of his working years in community development, and his primary passion was promoting physical activity for a healthy mind, body, and spirit.

Knowing what a difference sport made in his life at residential school, the disparities between the opportunities and facilities available to Indigenous and non-Indigenous youth frustrated him and motivated his political and social advocacy. He noticed these differences in every community he went to. He recalls addressing chief and council in Sandy Lake, the community of one of his former hockey teammates. Kelly was told that their priorities were housing, food, and clothing—not recreation. But because Kelly had lived for so long

Figure 14. The Prince Arthur hotel, similar to how it would have looked when Chris Cromarty and the Black Hawks stayed there in February 1951. 975.1.66 Prince Arthur hotel c. "before 1962." Used with permission from the Thunder Bay Museum.

The "Rocket" Meets the Sioux Lookout Indian Team

Maurice (Rocket) Rich-

out Indian School hockey team. The "Rocket" took part in last evening's Rendezvous by refer-

Figure 15. This newspaper clipping captures the moment when the Black Hawks met famed hockey player Maurice "The Rocket" Richard in what is now Thunder Bay in July 1951. Chris is third from the right (*front*). David is second from the left. Kelly is directly behind David, with the lower part of his face obscured. This is from an unknown newspaper but would have been either the *Fort William Daily Times-Journal* or the *Port Arthur News Chronicle*, and was found in a scrapbook of Gifford Swartman, former Indian Agent.

in the "white world," he had seen that communities like his adopted hometown of Timmins had multiple covered arenas as well as golf courses and track-and-field facilities. Why did Indigenous kids not have access to basic recreational facilities?

Kelly would go on to become a national figure in Indigenous sport development and take two groups of young Indigenous athletes to the North American Indigenous Games: in Blaine (a suburb of Minneapolis-St. Paul), Minnesota, in 1995 and Victoria, BC, in 1997. He often speaks of the joys of this period of his life and the immense responsibility of mentorship—the kind of support someone of his talent rightfully should have had during his own youth. As an example of the significance of his role, he draws on the memory of a young cross-country runner with whom he had only corresponded over the phone and through letters before they both arrived at the competition in Victoria:

> **Kelly:** A nice young man, oh he was. I was so glad to meet him. We had lunch together and we talked. Two days before he was to run, he came to me and said, "Kelly, I've got a problem. . . . You know, when I left my community, my grandma was very ill. And I just got a call from my mother and my grandma passed away. She wants me to come home and attend the funeral." Because apparently his grandma was one of the biggest supporters of what he was doing.
>
> **Alexandra:** Right.
>
> **Kelly:** "What do you think I should do, Kelly?" I said, "Well, you put in all those hours, those many days training, and your biggest supporter was your grandma! If I was you, I would run the race in her honour." . . . And you know, he stayed and ran and won a gold medal. And you know, even after the games were over, he would call me just to say hello. . . . It's those kinds of things you can't put a price tag on.

During his time working in community development, Kelly also consulted with remote and fly-in Indigenous communities about how to provide better recreational opportunities for their youth. As he explains, "I never abandoned the idea that play is good for the kids." He relates a pivotal moment of recognition at the first reserve he visited. Walking through the community, he saw a boy kicking a beer can down the road—his only form of recreation. This moment recalls the lengths to which Kelly and his peers went at Pelican Lake to fashion recreational activities. Kelly explained the process by which they would create makeshift ice-coated skis: "I guess some boys had saw somebody skiing somewhere, I don't know, on TV or a newspaper. But you know what we used to use as skis? We used to break [down] those used barrels and there would be pieces like this [gestures] and we'd sandpaper the one side and before we went to bed, we would water them down."

Beginning during his time at residential school, Kelly was aware of what he did not have. He often thinks of himself back in his bed at Pelican Lake at age six, living a far more "regimented" life than any child should. When reflecting on that time period and how it influenced him, he elaborates: "What I saw there, even as young as I was, [was that] youth—children—have this desire to want to *play*. . . . And I stood there on the side, scratched my cheek, and said, 'How come we don't have that opportunity here? Instead, we are out in the fields, fixing the gardens, hoeing the gardens, or cutting timber to heat the schools. That's not the way it's supposed to be.' I think slowly that thought stuck with me and I said, 'Well, there's going to have to be a change.'"

Later, Kelly somewhat contradicts himself in saying that he did not understand at the time that having to work all morning, to the point of being so tired he would fall asleep in class in the afternoon, was wrong. But both could be true. On one level, the experience of labouring to keep the school operational was normal because that was all he knew. Yet a part of him also understood that childhood should be different because he experienced love and freedom in his home community before being taken away to residential school. At Pelican Lake and later at Shingwauk, sports served as his escape from a reality that he could not control. He would "run away from all the negative," and excelled at any sport he tried.

It stands to reason, then, that the on-ice memories from the Southern Ontario tour would be the most vivid for Kelly. He does not remember swimming at the luxurious Chateau Laurier in Ottawa (see Figure 16 for a 1949 photograph of the hotel's pool). He does not remember meeting the dignitaries or presumably being chosen to shake the hand of the bishop, shown in Figure 17. But he does remember, in detail, the camaraderie between him and his fellow players on the ice. He often talks about playing defence with David in Toronto: "In nine seconds, they scored, Toronto. . . . I think it was one of the better midget teams. And I said, 'Oh, this is going to be a long night.' . . . And half of our team was midget, the other was bantam. But they were big and fast, oh boy."

Kelly has pride in the fact that although the opposing team was made up of older and bigger boys, the Black Hawks only lost by four goals. Considered one of the team's standouts, David scored the only goal for his team.

In addition to being a novelty, the Black Hawks were also great hockey players, which was part of their draw to the public. They were tough competition for the best Indigenous and non-Indigenous teams in their local area, such as the town of Sioux Lookout, and the region, such as the other residential schools McIntosh and Cecilia Jeffrey. According to Chris, and evidenced by the records, "we hardly ever lost." Winning was important; when I asked Chris if he was disappointed that he was not selected for the Southern Ontario tour, he replied that he was not, because "we were just anxious to win." The Black Hawks found that the hockey rink was one area in which they could demonstrate equality with, and potentially superiority to, the capabilities of their white peers. A competitive all-Indigenous drill team in Australia, the Cherbourg Marching Girls, recalled feeling a similar sense of racial pride and achievement when reflecting on a particularly memorable competition in the 1950s: "We weren't just the black fellas. . . . We ripped them and knocked them off their perch."[2]

However, demonstrating skills that rivalled their white competitors was not without consequence. Kelly recalled that he was subjected to poor treatment when he proved to be better than white players at

Figure 16. The swimming pool at the Chateau Laurier from around the time that the Black Hawks stayed at the hotel. 1949. ID Number X-30065. In public domain. Sourced from Ingenium.

Figure 17. Kelly Bull, flanked by his teammates and Pelican Lake's Principal Wilson, shakes the hand of the Bishop of Ottawa, Rev. Robert Jefferson. Photograph from the April 1951 tour. *Left to right, in foreground only, with full faces shown*: Frank Wesley, George Carpenter (side profile), Kelly Bull (shaking hand of Bishop), Johnny Yesno, Walter Kakepetum, and Bishop of Ottawa Rev. Robert Jefferson. Taken by NFB photographer Gar Lunney. #2AFC 451-S5-F14, 56955 6-5.2-27, 1950–1951. Archives and Special Collections, Western Libraries, Western University. Used with permission.

hockey or basketball later in life. When Kelly attended Shingwauk Indian Residential School for the older grades, he and Chris both played for the school's basketball team. Kelly was a standout player and his skills made him a target: he recalls "a lot of racism [and] comments: 'circle the wagon' and all that."[3] Kelly was also not given the opportunity to try out for the city's senior basketball team, which itself was later chosen to try out for Canada's Olympic team (Kelly believes that it was Shingwauk's principal who gave the order, wanting Kelly to concentrate on academics). David explained the complexities of being the only Indigenous player on the Port Arthur North Stars and the Port Arthur Bear Cats hockey teams, stating that he was sometimes teased and how it was uncomfortable to be the only "different" person on the team: "I had to be quiet," as there was no point in talking back. He further explained how once his teammates knew that he was a good player who would score goals and help them win, their minds changed, and they began to help him. Figure 18 shows David on the Port Arthur North Stars (bottom left).

Like in other settler colonial societies such as Australia and the United States, sports had a complex role in Canada. Many sports opportunities were provided by and promoted by the government with policy objectives in mind, but players also used sports to achieve their own goals.[4] Hockey provided rare moments of genuine fun, accomplishment, and mastery that were few and far between for the Black Hawks off the ice:

> **Chris:** [Hockey is] what occupied our time. Like I told you, hockey itself—it just kept our minds on hockey and didn't think much of anything else.
>
> **Alexandra:** It absorbed some of that negative feeling, negative energy.
>
> **Chris:** Even feeling lonely and lost. Even that kind of dissipates when you are having a lot of fun. Yeah.
>
> **Alexandra:** So, something to be excited about [and] to look forward to.

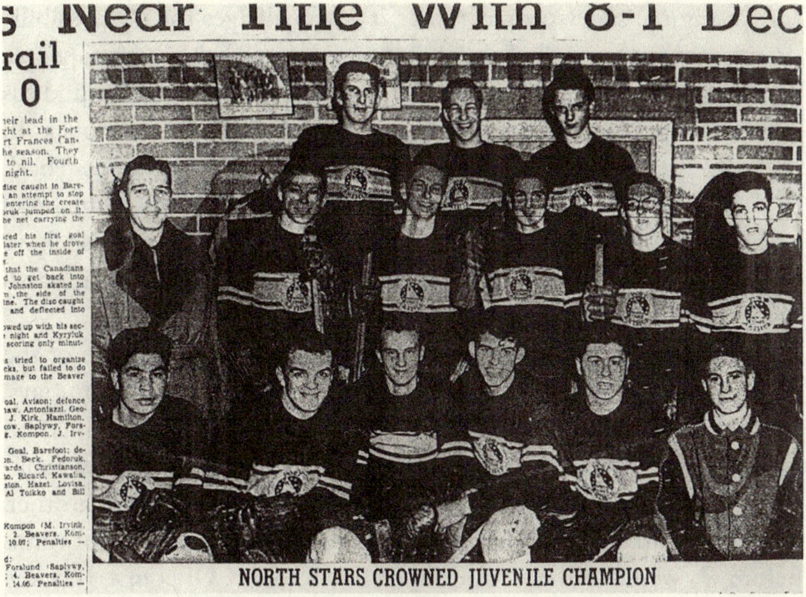
s Near Title With 8-1 Dec

rail
0

heir lead in the
ght at the Fort
rt Frances Can-
he season. They
to nil. Fourth
night.

disc caught in Bare-
an attempt to stop
entering the crease
oruk jumped on it,
he net carrying the

ored his first goal
later when he drove
e off the inside of

that the Canadians
d to get back into
Johnston skated in
n the side of the
ine. The disc caught
and deflected into

owed up with his sec-
night and Kyryluk
scoring only minut-

s tried to organize
cks, but failed to do
mage to the Beaver

oal, Avison; defence
haw, Antoniazzi, Geo-
J. Kirk, Hamilton,
cow, Saplywy, Fors-
g, Kompon, J. Irv-

Goal, Barefoot; de-
on, Beck, Fedoruk,
ards, Christianson,
to, Ricard, Kawalia,
ston, Hazel, Lovisa,
Al Toikko and Bill

Kompon (M. Irvink,
: 2, Beavers, Kom-
10.07; Penalties —

d:
Forslund (Saplywy,
; 4, Beavers, Kom-
14.06. Penalties —

NORTH STARS CROWNED JUVENILE CHAMPION

Figure 18. This newspaper clipping, newspaper unknown, shows the championship-winning hockey team that David Wesley played for upon moving to what is now Thunder Bay, called the Port Arthur North Stars, c. 1953. The clipping was shared with the research team by David Wesley and family.

> **Chris:** Yeah, that's right. And was it ever, as I can recall! Nothing else ever happened that shaped us like that.

Kelly recalls the team getting a private tour of Maple Leaf Gardens during the April 1951 tour and the awe he felt visiting the players' dressing room and getting to see and touch their multiple pairs of skates and their jerseys. Like the all-Indigenous Cherbourg Marching Girls, although their engagement with sport took place within vastly unequal power relations, sport also became a key part of community identity and was a source of pleasure and achievement.[5]

Hockey also allowed spaces for resistance. Researchers have explained that "recognizing Aboriginal agency does not discount the ways in which racism and oppression constrained choices and opportunities for Aboriginal sportspeople; rather, it acknowledges the . . . possibilities present in Aboriginal social discourse in which Aboriginal people are victors, not just victims."[6] Kelly recounted a story of him and his teammates playing hockey with mini-sticks and checkers for pucks in the hallways of the Chateau Laurier until their coach chased them back to their rooms (see Figure 19 for a photograph of rooms at the hotel around 1956). The boys had the rarest of opportunities to misbehave like other children on a school field trip without experiencing the harsh discipline that dominated their lives at Pelican Lake.

Chris remembers the thrill of sneaking out in the middle of the night to skate and of playing hockey for twelve hours on Saturdays, completely absorbed in the sport. "It took our minds off the situation we were in," he confirmed. "The most important thing for me about hockey: we were occupied. We didn't have time to bully each other. Tease each other. We didn't have time to be crooked. A lot of times before we were stealing food [out of hunger]. . . . Of course [hockey made us forget that we were hungry]. . . . We forgot a lot of things that were miserable about being in the residential school."

Kelly has a fond memory of skating on Pelican Lake, referring to Figure 20, in the years before they built the rink: "When we first started to entertain skating . . . there was lots of water around the school. In the fall times, that would freeze over and there'd be no snow. On a nice moonlit night, we'd go out and skate." The fact that hockey decreased student misbehaviour and introduced Indigenous children to the supposed benefits of white society was true. But the players' truth was that hockey was freedom.

Kelly: Was it fun and games or was there a deeper meaning?

Alexandra: Well, I have some ideas. But what do you think?

Kelly: I'd say both.

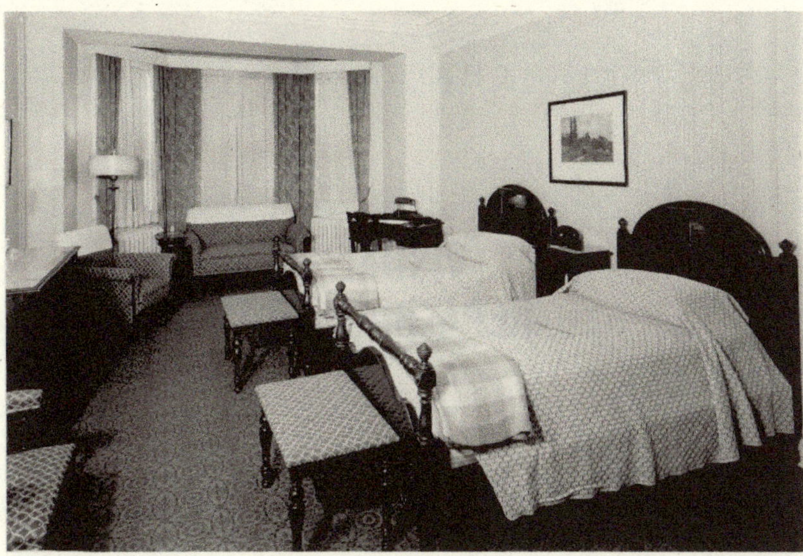

Figure 19. Dating to 1956, this photograph shows a typical hotel room at the Chateau Laurier, similar to what the Black Hawks would have stayed in during their 1951 tour. In public domain. ID Number X-40670. Sourced from Ingenium.

Figure 20. An aerial view of the residential school property that shows newly cleared land, the school, and a barn, c. 1927. P75-103, Item Number: S7-130. Used with permission from the Anglican Church of Canada, General Synod Archives Collection MSCC fonds.

CHAPTER 7

VISUAL REPATRIATION

Visual repatriation can provide an opening for stories that shed light on what has been hidden by colonial history. It challenges the one-dimensional and colonial historical imagery of Indigenous Peoples. Typically, visual repatriation involves returning images of ancestors and historical documents—often from museum collections—to source communities.[1] Such community-led and community-focused efforts to give these photographs new meaning create "counternarratives" to the official or mainstream historical narrative and are growing in popularity.[2] This involves asserting control over the histories associated with these photos and recasting the meanings of the pictures for their own purposes, thus enabling Indigenous Peoples to chart new futures.

The visual repatriation at the heart of this project gives photographs taken for very specific purposes new meanings born from decades of life experiences and from the fallout of public revelations about the internal workings of the residential school system. As an example, Kelly only much later learned that the Black Hawks' tour of Southern Ontario, of which he has generally fond memories, also served to improve the public image of residential schools, or, as he put it, to "make things look better." He commented on how innocent the boys were at the time. They could not have understood the broader motives for the hockey tour.

This project's visual repatriation reshapes the narrative that the NFB, in tandem with the DIA, told through the tour photos: that the Indigenous boys, guided carefully by the government's DIA administration, were embracing urban, modern Canada and leaving their cultural lifeways—and their status as distinct peoples—behind. This was the simple story in pictures that NFB photographer Lunney's camera lens communicated. The counter-story that the Black Hawks tell not only challenges the false impression suggested by the tour images, but also re-centres the survivors' narratives as truth-telling about what life was really like playing on the Black Hawks at Pelican Lake. In this way, their narratives become a restorying force that defies the idealistic portrayal of a harmonious Canadian nation that NFB photographs from this time period promoted.

Engagement with photos taken of themselves at residential school has allowed survivors from across the residential school system to "assert themselves as active remembering agents rather than archival objects."[3] Former students and their relatives made changes and additions to an exhibit of Anglican Church photos of students from Stringer Hall in Inuvik taken between 1964 and 1972. They corrected name misspellings, offered the students' Inuit names in place of their English names, and added family details to the exhibit with Post-it Notes. They identified students who had died and those who had become community leaders. Some of the Post-it Notes covered portions of the exhibit's text completely. The survivors and descendants of survivors literally rewrote the history that had been presented without their input.[4] This example demonstrates how "the photographic archive of residential schools is not a [straightforward] window onto the past, but, rather, a site of struggle shaped by ongoing colonial power."[5]

Important cultural insights can occur through engaging with historic photographs. In a study of Indigenous photo-sharing family gatherings conducted by Anishinaabekwe Celeste Pedri-Spade, one Elder recited the Anishinaabemowin (or Ojibwemowin) names of those pictured, which had been lost to assimilatory colonial naming practices. The family's descendants now had that information and part of their cultural knowledge "returned" to them.[6] An instance of Indigenous

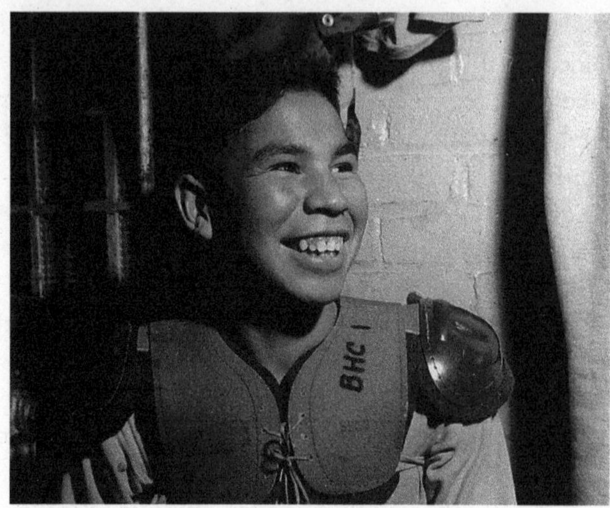

Figure 21. Portrait of David Wesley taken on the April 1951 tour. Taken by NFB photographer Gar Lunney. Source: AFC 451-S5-F14, 56965, 6-5.2-39, 1950–1951. Archives and Special Collections, Western Libraries, Western University. Used with permission.

peoples in both Canada and the U.S. reclaiming archival photos is Paul Seesequasis's sensitive rereading of photographs of Indigenous peoples in Northern Ontario.[7] Another important Canadian example of visual repatriation is the ongoing work of Project Naming. A collaboration between the Canadian government, universities, and an Inuit high school in Ottawa, this long-term program involves pairing Inuit youth with community Elders to identify ancestors and community members in historical government photographs from the 1940s to 1960s.[8] Copies of the photographs are offered to the Elders ("repatriated") and, more recently, have been used as the focal points for oral history interviews. In addition to inspiring the interviewers to be more engaged with their culture, these interviews have led to the formation of counternarratives about history and cultural practices that expand and challenge mainstream accounts of Inuit life.[9]

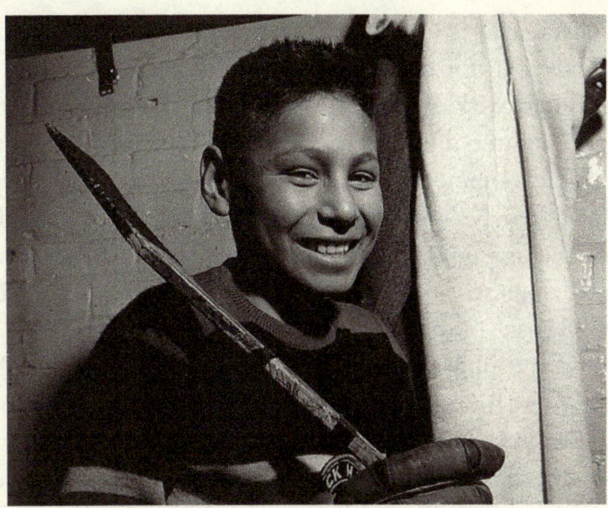

Figure 22. Portrait of Kelly Bull taken during the April 1951 tour. Taken by NFB photographer Gar Lunney. Source: AFC 451-S5-F14, 56964, 6-5.2-39, 1950–1951. Archives and Special Collections, Western Libraries, Western University. Used with permission.

Sharing these narratives about their residential school experiences, and especially about their time on the Black Hawks, can have an effect stretching beyond Indigenous communities and families to touch all people. Narratives create space for "a sense of ourselves as active participants in [the] world."[10] These narratives form the backbone of the Black Hawks' restorying work, work that can also serve to restore cultural and historical knowledge that was severed by the residential schools' assimilative project.

Visual repatriation projects assume that participants do not simply recall past events, but that they use photographs to explore and make sense of what the past means in the present, or how "we make sense of the past in our lived experience today."[11] David, Kelly, and Chris use the photographs to weave narratives that "[offer] us pasts which in one way or another reach into the present."[12] Reclaiming their histories and the telling of their stories is an "essential aspect of decolonization."[13]

For Kelly, David is forever a "rough-tough" hockey player and his fellow defenceman for the Toronto game of their 1951 tour. Having had little contact with each other throughout the intervening decades except for a laughter-filled afternoon during a chance encounter some years ago, Kelly's memories of David are more than seventy years old. Yet the affection in Kelly's voice was unmistakable when he said David's name upon seeing Figure 21. Looking at the photograph now, it is hard not to smile along with him. Kelly's portrait follows (Figure 22).

Figure 23 is one of the most reproduced images of the team. During an interview and photo elicitation session with David and his wife, Elise, their interactions with and about this photo brought home how visual repatriation can trigger strong emotions in present-day observers. Before offering comments on the picture in his hands, he passed it to his wife with a smile on his face and they laughed together. This warm exchange demonstrated their connection and love; looking at the image together also brought "those distant in space and time into the present."[14] Perhaps it was seeing the whole team together in a familiar image that caused David to reflect on what later became of the talented young hockey players. Of those in the photograph, he remarked on one teammate who experienced success. Most are now gone. As Kelly noted, many of them met sad ends after the long-term trauma of their years at residential school. But in that moment of holding the photo in his hands, for David, the struggles of the intervening years were less important than "seeing" them again, even through the prism of politically loaded imagery.

The photo elicitation process with David was fairly free flowing. David offered specific comments on only a handful of photos and much of the conversation between him, his wife, and Alexandra used the memories brought out by the photographs to offer reflections on that time in his life, the residential school system itself, and his later life up to the present. One of the images he specifically commented on was Figure 24: "I remember the totem pole."

This photograph is one of a handful taken of the players from the tour series at institutions of cultural importance in Ottawa. The exact

Figure 23. The Black Hawks (1951 or 1952) with personnel; *upper row, left to right*: Indian Agent Gifford Swartman, local businessman and volunteer Oreste Tintinalli, and local businessman and booster Art Schade. Players; *middle row, left to right (standing)*: Lawrence Carpenter, Albert Carpenter, Kelly Bull, Ernest Wesley, Agrippa Beardy. *Front row, left to right (kneeling)*: Frank Wesley, Chris Cromarty, Lawrence Beardy, David Wesley, Walter Kakepetum, Henry Spence, Angus Wesley. AFC 451–3/14.AFC 451-S5-F14, 6-5.2-30, 1950–1951. Reproduced with permission from Western Archives and Special Collections, Western University.

location of this photograph is not known; it was likely to have been taken at the National Museum. Though it is not possible to know exactly why this image was taken, it can be useful to consider what we have learned about photography of Indigenous people by outsiders. We can evaluate the image in light of the "before and after" genre that was commonly used in photographs promoting the residential school system. This one image seems to contain both elements: the totem pole signifying "before," and the modern boys in their hockey uniforms the

Figure 24. Three of the Black Hawks with Jan Eisenhardt, supervisor of physical education and recreation at the DIA, on their April 1951 tour. *Left to right*, Frank Wesley or David Wesley, Johnny Yesno, and Albert Carpenter. Taken by NFB photographer Gar Lunney. AFC 451-S5-F14, 56955, 6-5.2-27, 1950–1951. Reproduced with permission from Archives and Special Collections, Western Libraries, Western University.

"after." The way the photograph is staged, with Jan Eisenhardt seeming to be in the process of teaching the boys about the totem pole, and by extension about a homogenized version of Indigenous history, could also suggest that the Black Hawks were sufficiently separated from their culture that they now needed to learn about it in a museum as other Canadians did. If the totem pole symbolized the Indigenous past, the assimilated-seeming young men were the future envisioned by the Canadian government. In the eyes of the government, this future meant that Indigenous Peoples were to become simply another ethnic group in Canada's multicultural society, like Italians or Ukrainians, without treaty-based rights as distinct nations.[15] Figure 25[16] offers a similar scene. Photography continued to be a powerful method to communicate ideas about Indigenous Peoples.[17]

There might be significance in the fact that David remembered the totem pole. In a system where expressions of almost everything Indigenous were forbidden unless approved by white power brokers, getting to see an element of Indigenous culture, even one as non-specific as a totem pole, could have left a larger imprint in David's memory. This was certainly the case for Chris, who was not selected to join the Black Hawks on their 1951 Southern Ontario tour, but has strong memories of the team's tournaments in Fort William-Port Arthur (now Thunder Bay) in February and July of the same year. During the first interview and photo elicitation session, Chris had been certain that the team had only participated in one Thunder Bay tournament, in July, even though the initial archival evidence suggested that there had been two. The reason that he was so sure they had only visited once was because of his vivid memory of something that occurred while they were there: a Dominion Day parade where he saw Indigenous people marching in buckskin and feathered headdresses. He explained that "the reason I remember is that I saw, for the first time, Native people dressed in their regalia, because the Fort Williams [*sic*] First Nation was marching with the festivities there." This was the first time that he had seen Indigenous people wearing what he believed to be their ceremonial clothing "in real life."

A newspaper record from Tuesday, 3 July 1951, explained that the DIA-sponsored float bearing a reproduced teepee or wigwam had taken the top prize at the Dominion Day parade (Figure 26). Contrary to what the picture suggested—that Indigenous people had organized themselves to assert their culture through the parade—local First Nations' participation in the parade had been organized by the DIA. Instead of a contingent from the Fort William First Nation, "Indians in costume sat around a small fire atop the float. One carried her papoose on her back and the entire scene carried authentic reality."[18] But Chris did not seem disappointed that Indigenous participation in the parade was not exactly how he had remembered. The importance of seeing elements of Indigenous culture in public in July had, in fact, almost cancelled out the memories of the February tournament altogether.

Figure 25. The Black Hawks' April 1951 tour consisted of visits to institutions of civic importance. This photograph was taken at the Chateau Laurier. The mural, by C.W. Jefferys, was titled "Indians Paying Homage to the Spirit of Chaudiere." *Left to right*: Kelly Bull, David Wesley, unknown (*rear*), George Carpenter, Jerry Ross (*rear*), Ernest Wesley, Johnny Yesno, Walter Kakepetum, and unknown official. Taken by NFB photographer Gar Lunney. AFC 451-S5-F14, 56956, 6-5.2-27, 1950–1951. Archives and Special Collections, Western Libraries, Western University. Used with permission.

BLACK HAWKS

He explained the mix-up, saying "I made a mistake . . . because of [the parade during the July 1951 tournament] it was more clear in my head." Memories are not perfect reproductions of facts, but how the players reconstituted significant memories over time can tell us about their own aspirations and how they are using these remembrances to make sense of who they have become.

A by-product of their participation in hockey and leaving the school grounds was having the opportunity to be exposed to evidence of Indigenous culture and history, an aspect of their time on the Black Hawks that had resonance for Chris and David given the persistence of their memories up to the present. All three Black Hawks agreed that one of the main reasons why they enjoyed playing for the team so much was that it got them out of the school. As Chris explained, "When you're in the residential school, you never get out. You don't go travelling."

While the Black Hawks tour might have been planned to showcase the good work of the Anglican Church in the residential school system, the Black Hawks, like other Indigenous athletes, did not passively accept the administration's colonial sports agenda.[19] Seeing Indigenous people (Chris) and artifacts (David) meant that their cultures were not lost but had somehow endured. Perhaps these experiences helped them to make sense of the present moment and to imagine a different future, already planting the seeds of restorying.

What is shown in these images is not, for the most part, direct visual evidence of trauma. To put this another way, these photographs do not depict students being obviously mistreated. That truth was not photographed, either on their tour or in residential school history. Almost all official photographs taken of these schools and their students would have been undertaken with the intention of showing order, assimilation, good health, civilization, and the disciplined hard work of students in "manual training" or in the classroom; in other words, prosperity for the Canadian nation as a whole. These were the objectives that defined the purpose of the system and each institution within it.

The Daily Times-Journal

FORT WILLIAM, ONT., TUESDAY, JULY 3, 1951

EHEAD DOUBLED IN DECADE: FI

er to Dedicate Rendezvous Tonight

Seaway, R
Will Spark
Declares F

Indian Float Wins

All Fort William Out For Giant Procession

Twenty floats, eight bands and units of the Canadian (Reserve) Army were included in the mile-long parade yesterday which marked the opening of the three-day Fort William Rendezvous. The float section of the parade is shown in the above photo on North May Street.

Week-end Toll

12 Persons Injured In Traffic Mishaps

Figure 26. Newspaper clipping from the *Daily Times-Journal* (Fort William) from 3 July 1951. The float seen in the photograph ("Indian Float") is the one that Chris remembered so vividly.

Similarly, Project Naming's photographs, largely drawn from the NFB's Still Photography Division, reflect the federal government's agenda of promoting the North's economic potential. The agony of forced movement onto reserves and settlements, of children compelled into residential schools, and the overall end of traditional ways and land-based lifestyles are not evident in the photographs. What is largely seen is "Inuit assimilation in glowing terms."[20] In the same way, photographs taken aboard the HMS *Walnut*, a ship that transported hundreds of Estonian refugees to Canada in 1948—though in this case taken by passengers themselves—did not show the severe seasickness, the makeshift toilets, or the pain of being confined to a coffin-sized cubby for thirty-two days.[21] What becomes evident is that trauma is rarely depicted in photographs.

Participants in interviews using images from a traumatic period have reported, though, that the images can serve as a tool, or a buffer, to "speak through" while remembering and recounting these experiences.[22] Kelly and Chris certainly used the photographs in this manner. For David, discussing specific traumatic events was too painful. His comments reflect his approach to processing and coping with his residential school experiences, underpinned by his deep Christian faith: "There are a lot of Native people that won't forget, even though they are supposed to forgive. . . . It doesn't leave you. People don't forget what they've gone through. Sometimes it wants to come back [the bad memories] and I've gotta rebuke it."

In Alexandra's conversations around the photos, Chris and Kelly delved into other memories, even the traumatic and disturbing ones. Researchers have pointed out that many trauma survivors fear that people are not interested in listening to their stories or that they cannot find ways to tell their stories in a manner that makes them believable. In fact, "often the difficulty is not in remembering, but in communicating traumatic experiences as a reality."[23] An example from an interview with Kelly illustrates this point. Using a photograph of the school's cow barn, Figure 27, as an unlikely jumping-off point, Kelly recounted a troubling experience he had endured as part of the Indian Residential Schools Settlement Agreement claims process. Seeing the barn prompted him to emphasize how the children spent their time "shovelling cow shit [and] cleaning pig pens" instead of attending class. He added that he and his fellow survivors had been "taken to the cleaners on that point," meaning that he and the other claimants had not been fairly compensated for having been used as the main labour force for the school. In Kelly's eyes, the most offensive part of the claims process was not having been denied a larger sum of money, but that the harms he and others experienced were not fully recognized or accounted for. His trauma was not validated. Worse was that he had developed trust in his lawyer, even having him over

Figure 27. Cow barn at Pelican Lake Indian Residential School, 1948. Copyright expired. No restrictions on use. Online MIKAN no. 4673858. RG10. Volume/box number: 6503. Photographs. Library and Archives Canada. Item no. IND-13-1-94.

to the family home to work on their case, and now felt betrayed. The photograph of the cow barn proved to be an unexpected way to recount and process these traumatizing experiences.

Chris and Kelly were very deliberate in their comments and used our discussions around the photos to make broader statements about the destructive consequences of residential school on their own lives and their communities. Chris wanted to emphasize that what was depicted in the photographs of the 1951 tour had no relevance or meaning for struggling Indigenous communities: "Our parents never went to school; they didn't care about what was going on. They were trying to survive! Trying to survive. They didn't care about totem poles or Parliament buildings." The positive qualities he believes he was meant to learn from his family were wholly absent at Pelican Lake, despite what photographs might suggest. He explained: "You almost felt like a stranger every time you went home. And those . . . qualities that my parents had—my dad was a hard-working person to keep us all [with enough] food and clothing, and then my mother, as I told you, was a very caring person—you'd like to have those things, but nobody's teaching you them."

The survivors and their families struggle with the long-term repercussions of a system whose purpose included the deliberate breaking of family and community bonds in service of assimilation. Kelly recalled a conversation with his sister: "That's a statement my sister Jean floored me with one time when I was visiting in my early years [after school] in Winnipeg. You know, [she said] 'I never got to tell you I love you and that you were close to me. Because [in] residential school, they'd prevent that.' That kind of threw me for a loop. I guess, more than anything else, the love wasn't there." Chris also expressed that he felt like a stranger to his family every time he returned home from school—"like an alien" looking in.

It is crucial to bear in mind that in one major way, the residential school system failed. Though submerged and suppressed, the cultures of Indigenous children were not lost. What they could not express outright, they fought to keep in other ways, like how their home communities used "sports days" to engage in cultural activities. The Black Hawks remember speaking Ojibwemowin, on-ice, where they either could not be heard or could not be punished for it. Kelly explained that the grounds of the school were large enough and, in places, remote enough that he could continue to speak "in Indian" with his peers.

They recreated activities from their home communities such as hunting and fishing, some with the official encouragement of the school, and some self-directed and under the radar. Trapping, to which students gravitated, helped to pay down the Black Hawks' tour debt and occasionally provided the boys with a bit of pocket money. Kelly recalls that one Saturday, after checking the traps set the week before, "Everyone came back with long faces except Walter. Walter caught a mink!"

The boys used their knowledge from home about how to gather firewood, build a fire, and cook what they had caught. They also drew upon what they had learned in their home communities about the habits of animals, according to Kelly. Their Indigenous supervisor and hockey coach, Pete Seymour, helped to fill in the blanks with skills that they should have learned at home but did not have the opportunity to. He instructed them in setting snares and would take them to the rapids and explain that this was where the minks usually forage for dead animals. Kelly elaborated on these moments of temporary freedom:

> Boys would go fill their pockets with . . . little pebbles and go in the bush and hunt for partridge. And they would come out with some partridges, clean them up, wash them, put a skewer through [them], and cook them that way. That was a good time—you know, for us, it was almost like the pressure was released. We were out where we should be, you know. Well, the supervisors always had the whistle: "Tweet!" That meant come on back to the railroad bridge to start walking back to school. But those were good times. We were away from the pressure, and we were in the bush and breathing fresh air and laughing, only to be pushed back into reality.

From the bridge mentioned and pictured here in Figure 28, he remembers snaring suckers: "On Saturday afternoons when we weren't hauling logs or hauling coal, we'd go for a walk down to the track and head towards Sioux Lookout on the tracks and about half a mile there was a [railroad] bridge. . . . I think it was that Indian guy [Pete Seymour] that was supervising, so he didn't really mind us building a fire to cook the fish. There were *those* times that I remember."

For Kelly, recounting the exuberance and freedom he felt being outdoors and on the land connected him to his pre-residential-school childhood when he spent many happy days picking and processing wild rice with his *kokum* (grandmother). This is one of many stories that Kelly tells from his life before Pelican Lake that is intended to counter the misconception that Indigenous children were not being educated in their home communities. Learning about changes to

Figure 28. The bridge from which Kelly and his peers snared fish, 1950. From Archives and Special Collections, Western Libraries, Western University. Used with permission.

the land and animal behaviour patterns, learning to care for others in their clan, learning which plants were edible, learning around the fire from the teachings of the older ones—"that was all education. It didn't come from books." He recalls being taught right from wrong, to live by the principles of the Seven Grandfather Teachings, and how to prepare plant medicines that had analgesic effects. Kelly takes offence to the very premise of the residential school system because it assumed that Indigenous parents were unwilling or unable to educate their children. As his examples make very clear, in his home community "there was teaching there. You didn't have to go to the classroom to learn." This type of holistic teaching was embedded into his everyday life at home through an Ojibwe worldview:

> [My father] didn't say, per se, "this is what you've gotta be to survive in this maddening world." He knew. And that's the way Indian teaching was. Like even my Grandma Sapay, my *kokum*. She wouldn't say "Now pay attention." She'd do it by action. . . . "Sit down, be quiet, watch."

> That was how you were instructed. *Bizindan*. That means "listen." And there were some comparisons to the animal world, too. . . . That's that part that was cut off when I went to residential school. Boom. That kind of learning went by the wayside. But what I *did* learn [at home]—I found it very invigorating, and it made a lot of sense to me, and then, poof! Put into this strange world!

Kelly wrestles with how institutional life changed him and his fellow students. It was worlds away from the kinship-based system of mutual support that many of them had experienced in their home communities. Instead of sharing treats that lucky students who received money from their parents purchased from the school's canteen, they kept the snacks for themselves: a "viciousness" that never would have been tolerated at home. Kelly was surprised at these non-hockey-specific memories that bubbled to the surface over the course of many conversations: "Initially, I thought we would be only talking about recreation—but that was life at the residential school."

In Chris' words, hockey was maybe the most exciting thing that ever happened to them at school, but it was not the only thing. The proper context, as they saw it, included the daily humdrum existence of life at Pelican Lake. Chris put it this way:

> **Chris:** That's not the whole story because there were other things happening other than hockey.
>
> **Alexandra:** Of course.
>
> **Chris:** The way the living conditions were. All the direction. We're doing the same thing every day. Three meals a day. Three churches on Sunday. Going to bed at seven. Getting up at seven. All that kind of stuff. Doing chores on our hands and knees. They didn't have mops as we have now, so you had to get on your knees with a scrub brush.

In the interview sessions with the Black Hawks, particularly with Kelly and Chris, they were eager to identify their fellow players and classmates in the photographs. While this may seem like an obvious way to engage with a photograph, consider that few residential school survivors have access to photographs of themselves from those formative years or even know that photographs of them at school might exist. Naming was a key tool of colonization in Canada. Indigenous places and nations were often given English names. Indigenous children were commonly renamed when baptized or when entering residential school. "Kelly" in his community was called Quiwi. "Chris" was given as a baptismal name. Kelly expressed frustration when he could not remember the name of a peer, despite being able to identify many others: "I should know him. He's always got the same expression." On the other hand, he was very pleased to be able to confidently say of Figure 29, "Yeah, that's [my brother] George, alright," who he also identified by his Ojibwe name. Chris could identify the home communities and possible relatives of some of those pictured.

In many Indigenous traditions, a name has more than mere sentimental value. Naming a child is often quite purposeful, and names could be chosen to commemorate a beloved or admired ancestor, to express kinship relations, or to indicate one's role in the community. In the same way that restoring Indigenous place names is important for decolonization, so too is naming—and, by extension, remembering and humanizing—the many anonymous faces in residential school photographs. As we flipped through the photographs and the players were named, so too were they humanized by the details the three survivors remembered. When asked if he remembered a specific player shown, Chris responded: "Albert Carpenter. He was the captain of the team. He's a skater." David proudly recalled how another one of his teammates, Johnny Yesno, had gone on to become a successful actor and radio host. The Black Hawks' focus on each other, not on the "important" politicians and officials they met, mirrors Sami and Inuit recollections prompted by historic photographs. The Sami, who were undertaking visual repatriation with images from Norwegian schools, were single-mindedly focused on their fellow pupils, asking, "Who they were, what kinds of homes or environments they come from, what happened to them?"[24] The Inuit who commented on images of their community members taken during the Governor General's 1956 tour of their territory likewise emphasized their kin and ignored the "important" government official.[25] In his comments on a photograph from the tour featuring one of the players shaking the hand of a dignitary (Figure 17), Kelly ignored the latter altogether, instead remarking, "And there's little Albert! He could skate like the whirlwind, that kid. There he is." He praised another teammate, Matthew Strang, saying, "I've never seen a kid that was as acrobatic as he was!" Residential school had stripped the students of their individual identities, so the act of naming them—and their singular qualities—reclaims an important part of who they are and where they come from.

The importance of naming those in these historic photographs—either giving names to unnamed persons or correcting existing records—has been a key aspect of other visual repatriation efforts. Though long-term efforts of organizations such as the Shingwauk Centre have identified students in residential school photographs, the identities of countless others are waiting to be reclaimed. The work of Project Naming, mentioned above, has been transformative in its ability to restore the identities and kinship connections of those photographed by government agencies in the Arctic. Before this project, most of the photographs in the Library and Archives Canada collections presented Inuit as anonymous "types," such as "Native woman, Pond Inlet, Baffin Island, N.W.T." After engaging with community Elders using these photographs, the caption was retitled to now read "Miali Aarjuaq wearing an 'amauti' (a woman's hooded caribou parka). This photograph was taken near the R.C.M.P. Detachment."[26] The presentation of non-white people as anonymous racial "types" through photography has deep historic echoes.

Additionally, photographs of the Black Hawks on tour were consistent with other residential and boarding school images that showed the supposed benefits of assimilation. In Figure 30, twelve Indigenous boys in matching jackets are shown eagerly learning from

Figure 29. Kelly identified his brother George in this photograph, c. 1950. Reproduced with permission from Shingwauk Residential Schools Centre (Algoma University). From an album of photographs that belonged to former Pelican Lake staff member Joyce Clinton.

Figure 30. The Black Hawks at the National Archives in Ottawa during their April 1951 tour. *Left to right, front row, seated*: George Carpenter, Frank Wesley, Ernest Wesley, possibly Dominion Archivist W. Kaye Lamb, Johnny Yesno, Jerry Ross, and Walter Kakepetum. *Left to right, top row, crouching or standing*: Kelly Bull, David Wesley, Henry Spence, Matthew Strang, Eddie Mandamin, and Albert Carpenter. Taken by NFB photographer Gar Lunney. AFC 451-S5-F14, 56953, 6-5.2-27, 1950–1951. From Archives and Special Collections, Western Libraries, Western University. Used with permission.

a seemingly important white man in what appears to be a library. They are posed with items that indicate "civilization," such as books strategically placed in the foreground of the image, with care not to block any of the boys' attentive faces. Figure 31 shows the boys—this time smiling—photographed in front of Parliament's centre block main doorway, a recognizable symbol of the nation of Canada and suggestive of the boys' development as citizens.

A photograph of the Black Hawks taken having supper with government officials in Parliament on their 1951 tour, Figure 32, calls up similar themes. At the end of the table seated on the right-hand side is Paul Martin Sr., then Minister of National Health and Welfare. The photograph shows the players in the very centre of Canadian government and nation, eating at, in David's words, a "white people's table" where he recalls that some players were so nervous that their hands were shaking. According to Kelly, the boys received etiquette lessons in the train's dining car on their way to Southern Ontario.

Similar to the Cherbourg Marching Girls' tours throughout southeastern Australia, the Black Hawks' tour portrayed "positive perceptions of assimilation exemplifying the benefits of cultural uniformity, demonstrating equality of opportunity, and promoting prosperity for those who were willing to adopt settler values and ideas."[27] Crucially, though, Kelly made it clear that the boys did not know that attempts to assimilate them were being made through the tour: "That's just our innocence. We just liked to play the game. We liked to skate. . . . To attach a political meaning to it—I don't think we ever thought that."

Over the course of our years-long collaboration, Kelly's perspective on the images of the Black Hawks changed. Kelly more forcefully questioned what he saw in the images and the players' unwitting participation in a photographic campaign for the system that they despised. As a child he could not understand the hockey tour's political motivations. Now, in his own words, he sees how "the government was trying to tell the public that the Indian kids were happy. Look at the smiles on their faces."

Figure 31. The Black Hawks watch an unnamed official, possibly MP for Fort William Daniel McIvor, play a musical instrument at Parliament (the House of Commons) during their 1951 tour. Taken by NFB photographer Gar Lunney. AFC 451-S5-F14, 56968, 6-5.2-37, 1950–1951. From Archives and Special Collections, Western Libraries, Western University. Used with permission.

To viewers today, these photographs and others from the collection are quite obviously "posed." Yet Chris, David, and Kelly do not recall much about their experiences being posed. Like the others, Chris has vivid memories of his time on the team and of their tournaments generally, but does not remember much about the specific moments captured in photographs. The day after Alexandra first interviewed Kelly, he explained that he had been mulling over what he had learned the previous day: "I laid in my bed this morning, trying to think of, do I recall ever a photographer being in the room? But maybe he was

Figure 32. The Black Hawks have dinner at Parliament during their April 1951 tour. The players are, from foreground to background on the left side of the table: Henry Spence, George Carpenter, Frank Wesley, Jerry Ross, and Albert Carpenter. On the right side from background to foreground with faces in view: Eddie Mandamin, Walter Kakepetum, David Wesley, and Johnny Yesno. Taken by NFB photographer Gar Lunney. AFC 451-S5-F14, 56957, 6-5.2-27, 1950–1951. From Archives and Special Collections, Western Libraries, Western University. Used with permission.

unannounced, and he was not conspicuous. He [might have said], 'Oh, I'm going to take some pictures for Mr. Martin's scrapbook,' or something to that effect."

Always keen to look beneath the surface, Kelly added, "The greater meaning of that is that they were setting us up for something. Well, I don't know, maybe that's kind of harsh." Kelly had a hard time coming to terms with the fact that the players were "manipulated" in this way, in part because he has such positive memories of sports at residential school. In a follow-up session, hinting at how "the whole story" of the

Black Hawks must include the ordeals of life at the school outside of hockey, he explained how he was making sense of this new information:

> **Kelly**: What threw me for a loop, too, [was] when Janice said we were made to be that way.
>
> **Alexandra**: Mm-hmm. You were posed.
>
> **Kelly**: Yeah, posed.
>
> **Alexandra**: How did it throw you for a loop—it made you reconsider something?
>
> **Kelly**: It did something to me. It wasn't natural. But I didn't know I was being manipulated . . . to look happy instead of being sad.
>
> **Alexandra**: And that's how you see it now?
>
> [**Kelly** sighs heavily].
>
> **Kelly**: Yeah, I guess to a certain extent.

One of David's few remarks specifically related to a photo centres on being posed. Regarding Figure 33, he said, "they had to teach us how to sit down like that." David is in the front row at the far left. Another of his later comments touches on the artificial nature of some parts of the tour in comparison to their everyday lives at Pelican Lake: "They never used to buy us new things. I don't know where they got those jackets." The tour, and the image that the tour portrayed to the public, was vastly different than the rest of the boys' lives at school.

Pictures of the past are, quite obviously, a historical source and artifact, but they are also "social things."[28] They can carry real pain and have effects on present-day social interactions and relationships. The pain on David's face was evident when he looked at photographs that caused him to remember the abuse that one of his classmates endured. Yet, looking at the photograph in a vastly different context than that in which it was produced—now in his living room with his wife, with decades separating the present moment from that

Figure 33. The Black Hawks pose with Jan Eisenhardt in Ottawa on their April 1951 tour. *Top row, left to right*: Eddie Mandamin, Jerry Ross, Albert Carpenter, Jan Eisenhardt, Frank Wesley, Walter Kakepetum, and Henry Spence. *Bottom row, left to right*: David Wesley, Ernest Wesley, Kelly Bull, Johnny Yesno, Matthew Strang, and George Carpenter. Taken by NFB photographer Gar Lunney. #1AFC 451-S5-F14, 56960 6-5.2-27, 1950–1951. From Archives and Special Collections, Western Libraries, Western University. Used with permission.

time—the image was "re-established with different frames."[29] A different narrative emerged, and a different story was told, one with a much different ending than its beginning. David explained that as an adult, his classmate eventually challenged his abuser in court: "You gotta watch. People that really mistreat people—they remember."

In the context of anthropometric photography—photographs that anthropologists took to provide physical data of different racial "types"—part of the reason these images are so compelling today is the contrast between the objectification of the subjects and the evidence of their humanity: as scholar Edwards explains, an "awareness of 'beyond' that is part of [their] power."[30] When David looked at that photograph, taken during an especially oppressive time in Indigenous history, and spoke about the later triumphs of his classmate who had been abused, he reclaimed the narrative and captured the "beyond" that Edwards describes.

The survivors' present-day engagement with photos from their time at residential school served to elicit stories that captured the depths of their intelligence and resiliency. Looking at the images in conversation with Chris led to a profound understanding of what sports had meant to him during that dark, lonely period. He first heard Foster Hewitt announcing a Toronto Maple Leafs vs. New York Rangers game through the staticky radio in the supervisor's bedroom at Pelican Lake. Knowing that there was a whole world extending beyond the confines of the institution, symbolized by hockey in distant cities, allowed him to be able to survive those terrible years. He remarked that after hearing that first broadcast, "you find out in geography studies that [New York City] is supposed to be one of the largest cities in the world, so that kind of leads into all that from this experience we had with hockey." As a young adult, Chris loved attending hockey games in Toronto, where he was working, and had gone to New York City for his first-ever vacation. It is fitting that when the research team asked him to select a handful of images about his life, he chose one from the top of the Empire State Building. June 10, 2022, marked the end of his earthly journey, and as a testament to

Figures 34a and b. Photograph (front and back) of Chris Cromarty as a young man visiting New York City. Given to authors by Chris Cromarty and used with permission.

Chris's spirit, we have included the photo and his witty caption on the back (Figures 34a and b): "Photo taken at top of Empire State Building at New York City in October 1958. *P.S. I was a mid-day cowboy way before Jon Voight was a mid-night cowboy."

EPILOGUE

PICTURING THE FUTURE

BY ALEXANDRA GIANCARLO

It is a blisteringly hot August morning in Ottawa. On the way back from having a coffee, a friend and I encounter an elderly man standing near his SUV, looking slightly lost. It is a quiet day in the sleepy residential neighbourhood, and Joe explains to us that he had been trying to reach an administrator at the school in front of which we're standing. School, though, is not yet back in session, and after we suggest that Joe return in September, he hands us the photo and begins to explain. It is a blown-up image, crisp despite its evident age, showing a black-and-white elementary-school-age boys' hockey team. The 1950s. Though the boys are not posed quite as stiffly as the Black Hawks were in their images, the overall effect is similar enough. Lightheartedly, Joe asks us to pick him out in the photograph, and my friend does so successfully, pointing to a slick-haired boy in the front row, a reverse-aged facsimile of the elderly man standing in front of us. As these photographs so often do, this one prompted Joe to share stories about what became of the smiling boys in the team photo, who were local champions. Most of them lost touch when they moved on to high school. One or two had gone on to be excellent sportsmen in their high school years. One later worked for law enforcement in the city of Ottawa. The photograph captured a fleeting moment in time, but one that Joe valued so much that he was, today, attempting to give the image back to the school that they had all attended, and played for, more than seventy years ago.

To not draw parallels between these hockey players and the Black Hawks is impossible. Because both sets of posed images conform to the photographic conventions of the 1940s and the 1950s, the photographs of the Black Hawks and of Joe's team are, in a way, ordinary. Some would have ended up in the sports pages of the local newspaper, as was commonly done during this time period. Countless similar images would have been proudly displayed on refrigerators, saved in a scrapbook, or lovingly tucked into a family Bible—as Chris's mom did with his team photo. And despite lives and experiences vastly different to those of Joe and his teammates, Chris, Kelly, and David metaphorically hold out their team photos as if to say, "We were here. We mattered."

Though government policy shaped their hockey experiences, the boys were not passive. Hockey became a lifeline, almost in a literal sense, as it was a refuge from the abuse and neglect the boys faced. Hockey was their resistance—a force that resulted in a tiny crack in the powerful structure of the residential school system through which a sliver of light could be let in. It temporarily stilled the monotony of the taxing physical labour to which they were subjected, redirected and quieted bullies' anger, and offered genuine pride and satisfaction in their physical abilities. Their triumph over white teams to become local and regional champions brought individual and collective pride, as other residential school survivors have expressed.[1] Yet as we know now from the administrative correspondence and policy documents of the time period, officials saw sports as a way to reinforce the residential school agenda by improving overall discipline and decreasing student misbehaviour (most notably truancy, one of the primary ways that students expressed their dissatisfaction).

The images of the boys playing hockey could be seen as evidence that something positive did happen at residential school. But to use these images to frame their experiences as "good" ignores what they obscured, both at the time and in what came after. Some of the Black

Hawks had died "horrible deaths," as Kelly says, mere decades after leaving school, spat out by a colonial system that annihilated their identities as Indigenous people, yet left them unequipped to survive in the white Canadian world.

These photographs allowed the Anglican Church, and the Canadian government, to be able to publicly cling to the fiction that residential school students were receiving educational and extracurricular experiences on par with—and perhaps exceeding—those of mainstream society's youth. Nothing could have been further from the truth. While Joe spoke casually about his peers attending secondary school, whether that meant a technical, commercial, or collegiate institution, in 1956 only 136 students in the DIA schools had reached grade twelve. This figure was less than one percent of the total enrolled students.[2] The survival, and relative successes, of Kelly, Chris, and David are the exception. By definition, they are the ones who must tell the story of themselves and the others if it is to be remembered.

During our last meeting, Chris and his wife, Annie, had presented me with an intricately beaded necklace, one that Annie had made years ago, before her eyesight and manual dexterity declined. The necklaces—one each for Janice and me—had different imagery woven into their strands, such as a fire, a beaver, a bow and arrow, and other symbols. Chris mentioned that these were part of a collection. A handful remained back home in Wunnumin Lake. The beaded patterns of images, he explained, helped him to remember some of the traditional stories and legends, because the written versions no longer existed. These necklaces, therefore, were both historical items and repositories of stories.[3]

Something similar could be said about the hockey photographs: that they were objects of history but also held histories. Like the necklaces, the photographs' corresponding written history is minimal—at best, lopsided, favouring the official narrative put forth by the Anglican Church, the DIA, and the NFB's Still Photography Division. When Chris looked at the necklaces, he told me that they helped him to remember the important parts of the story. When Chris gave the necklaces to me and Janice, yet another chapter was added to their stories. For the Black Hawks, the photographs did offer a window into their shared past. But part of the gift of the hockey images has been that engaging with them has offered the players new insights, complexities, and ways to come to grips with telling their complicated histories. The Black Hawks' engagement with these images stretched all the way back to the Doctrine of Discovery, as Kelly wrestled with the inhumanity of colonialism. Like the necklaces, the re-circulation of the images in today's context opens a new chapter in their story, one that is still being written.

To David, it is significant and something of a reckoning that his daughter graduated from the same school the players attended, now under Indigenous control as Pelican Falls First Nations High School. David and his family have expressed hope that this book and this story will help people and build understanding. Chris spent much of his adult life working for Indigenous people as one of the founders of Treaty 9's Nishnawbe Aski Nation; perhaps his proudest legacy is the many foster children he and his wife have parented. Kelly often says that the responsibility for change towards justice for Indigenous Peoples, and for making a better world for his granddaughter, is now in the hands of the next generation. In the final season of their lives, the restorying, and restoring, work of the Black Hawks helps to heal the past, give new meaning to the present, and provide strength for the future.

ACKNOWLEDGEMENTS

Crafting history is never a solitary venture. As authors, the stories we end up telling originate from the minds and hearts of many different people, who each come to the table with their own point of view. In the end, what finally gets told is an intricate compilation of their perspectives and experiences, including our own as lead authors. Here, we have fused together multiple histories to "make sense" of our past, as individuals and as a society. Indigenous histories are fertile grounds where we are forced to grapple with the stories we tell to ourselves and others.

This story became richer and more detailed through a coincidental encounter between Janice Forsyth and Jan Eisenhardt, whom Indian Affairs hired in 1950 as their first Supervisor of Physical Education and Recreation. His job was to use sports and games to speed up the process of Indigenous assimilation in the Indian residential school system and on reserves throughout Canada. One of Jan's projects was to organize the hockey tour for the Sioux Lookout Black Hawks in 1951. When Jan resigned from Indian Affairs in early 1952, frustrated with this mandate and the resources he was given to support sports and recreation activities throughout the country, he walked away with most of his files and kept them in his basement at home in Dorval, Quebec. In Jan's files there were the same, original photographs of the Black Hawks that Kelly had in his box at home, along with official correspondence, Jan's own journaling, photographs, news clippings, posters, and other memorabilia of the tour. His archive helped us understand why the tour was organized. When Jan passed away in 2004, his daughter, Lisa Spillane, became the family historian. Later, she donated Jan's files to

Western University's Archives and Special Collections, where they can be accessed as AFC 451. As a person of historical importance, being appointed to the Order of Canada and Canada's Sports Hall of Fame, Jan is recognized, and his story is told in many other places. Notably, he is one of the main subjects of *The Un-Canadians*, a documentary that chronicles the lives of people who were blacklisted for alleged communist sympathies during the Cold War era. His work at Indian Affairs also forms the basis of *Reclaiming Tom Longboat: Indigenous Self-Determination in Canadian Sport*. Jan maintained a fervent belief that sports and physical activities had the "power" to help people to understand one another. Although he worked for Indian Affairs, he was not a "company man" by any stretch of the imagination; he would have wanted the Black Hawks to tell this story.

The "heart" of this story revolves around three individuals, whose insights—in helping us to understand what version of their past they wanted to tell—are infused into every page of this book.

Chris Cromarty generously shared of himself throughout the many years that this project has been underway. As the idea of a book began to take greater shape and Alexandra was brought on as a postdoctoral associate, she and Chris met twice in Thunder Bay before Covid-19 hit. Chris remained dedicated to the project and its vision as he and Alexandra navigated continuing this work through the mail, over crackly phone lines, and through Covid-cautious visits. During the final visit before his passing, Chris expressed his enduring wish that the Black Hawks story would shed light on the damage that the residential school system wrought on individuals, communities, and Indigenous ways of life. Chris also explained that he admired the cultural strength of his wife, Annie, who had not attended residential school. Yet Chris was equally strong, and someone whom Alexandra, in turn, admired for his determination to begin to heal himself decades after leaving Pelican Lake.

Kelly Bull brought this story to light over a cup of tea in the early 2000s as he was reflecting on what would become of Canada's attempt to address its injustice. Now well into his 80s, he has moved from the home he shared in Timmins, Ontario with his beloved wife Greta, who has since passed on to the spirit world, to live with his son in British Columbia. Geographically, he is far away from his home community in Obizhigokaang (Lac Seul First Nation) in northern Ontario but remains committed to their survivance from afar.

Kelly has written the following:

> This is for all of my teammates, the vast majority of them are in the Spirit World. We were stronger together.
>
> I can never repay my mom and dad for their strength and determination to raise a family of seven children in colonial conditions made immeasurably harder by the flood.
>
> This is especially for my *kokum*, Annie Sapay—without her I would be lost. She took on the role of mother when my own mother was in a sanitorium with tuberculosis a province away (not to be seen again by me for over twenty years). My *kokum*'s unbreakable spirit and gentle way of teaching connected me to an earlier time and gave me the fortitude to endure what was to come. Her kindness is what inoculated me to total despair and rage and, in my twenties, eventually allowed me to open my heart to Greta—the woman who would become my wife and the mother of our children. Without Greta's wisdom, I would never have reconciled with my mother. [Greta] brought song, humour, and the compassion of a nurse into the life we made together. Gone for over seven years now, I talk to her every day.
>
> And to the ray of light that is my granddaughter, Macy. This is for you.

David Wesley would like to thank Kelly Bull, Black Hawks' coach-supervisor Pete Seymour, the other Survivors, his son Brad for his interest and help with telling his story, and the academic team responsible for this book.

Several other people helped to assemble the backdrop to this story. Together, they comprise the larger research team that was a sounding board for ideas and carried out specific projects to advance this work. Fatima Ba'abbad completed her Master's thesis that provided valuable insight on key themes, as well as practical matters, such as how to combine oral history interviews with photographs to elicit conversations about "big ideas" like coloniality and survivance. Prior to Alexandra joining the team in 2019, Evan Habkirk helped us to navigate the complicated world of archival data collection, leading one memorable research trip to the Library and Archives Canada and the old Department of Indian Affairs archives in Ottawa. Taylor McKee's insight on hockey culture is unrivaled; his observations about who was in the photographs, the quality of the Black Hawks' uniforms and sticks, the language used in the newspaper reporting, and so on showed us how important this trip was for the church and state. Sam Cronk and Gavin Bennett rounded out our "motley crew" with their interest in representational issues, with Sam's experience in museum studies and Gavin's in library and information sciences. There were many angles from which to approach this story—this book is the result of their collective input.

Many archives were consulted, sometimes multiple times, including the Western Archives and Special Collections, Library and Archives Canada, the National Art Gallery of Canada, Shingwauk Residential School Centre at Algoma University, the Archives of Ontario, the Anglican Diocesan of Toronto Archives, and the National Film Board of Canada Archives in Montreal. Thank you to all of the archivists, assistants, and others who fielded our seemingly boundless queries.

Thank you to everyone at the University of Manitoba Press, where Jill McConkey, Barbara Romanik, Sarah Ens, David Larsen, Stephanie Paddey, and Kyla Neufeld shepherded our book through this process with great attention and care.

Alexandra would like to thank her friends, parents, brother, "lifetime adventure partner" Mike, her in-laws and brother-in-law, beloved kitties Rascal and Jingles (R.I.P.), and extended family who were steadfast in their support for and interest in this project. Heartfelt thanks, with deep affection, to the Survivors and their families: Kelly, Richard, Lori, and Alpine Bull; David and the Wesley family, especially sons Brad and David (Tom); and Chris and Annie Cromarty. Thank you to Niiyokamigaabaw Deondre Smiles, Dalia Edwards, and Dene Sinclair and the AICHO language table for their cultural insights, and to Douglas Semple and Chris Winnepetonga for their assistance facilitating community connections. Alexandra would also like to thank her co-authors Braden and Janice. A special note of appreciation goes out to Janice as a mentor and for seeing my potential to undertake research with Indigenous communities with thoughtfulness and sensitivity. Thank you for welcoming me into these relationships and into a robust research group!

Janice extends her heartfelt thanks to Kelly Bull for sharing his story with her all those years ago and for continuing to walk this journey alongside her and everyone who has contributed to bringing this story to life—especially Alexandra and Braden, whose unwavering understanding of its significance nurtured and sustained our commitment to getting it done.

In addition to the acknowledgements noted above Braden wishes to thank his family, and in particular his wife and children. I tautoko a Braden i ngā mihi i mihia, ā, ka tukua ngā mihi nui, ngā maioha ki te whānau, otirā, ko Jenn, rātou ko a māua tamariki, ko Liliana, ko Kyla, ko Gracie. Nā rātou ahau i tauwhiro, nā rātou ahau i whakaaweawe. Tēnā koutou.

We also gratefully acknowledge the support of the Social Sciences and Humanities Research Council Grant, Insight Grant (435-2016-0713) and the Western University Doctoral Fellowship Program for providing much needed resources to carry out this work.

NOTES

Preface

1 Janice Forsyth, "Bodies of Meaning: Sports and Games at Canadian Residential Schools," in *Aboriginal Peoples and Sport in Canada: Historical Foundations and Contemporary Issues*, ed. Janice Forsyth and Audrey R. Giles (Vancouver: UBC Press, 2013), 16.

2 Fatima Ba'abbad, "History of Sioux Lookout Black Hawks Hockey Team, 1949–1951" (Master's thesis, University of Western Ontario, 2017); Braden Paora Te Hiwi, "Physical Culture as Citizenship Education at Pelican Lake Indian Residential School, 1926–1970" (PhD diss., University of Western Ontario, 2015).

3 Alexandra Giancarlo, Janice Forsyth, Braden Te Hiwi, and Taylor McKee, "Methodology and Indigenous Memory: Using Photographs to Anchor Critical Reflections on Indian Residential School Experiences," *Visual Studies* 36, no. 4–5 (2021): 406–20, https://doi.org/10.1080/1472586X.2021.1878929.

4 Forsyth, "Bodies of Meaning"; Janice Forsyth and M. Heine, "'The Only Good Thing that Happened at School': Colonising Narratives of Sport in the Indian School Bulletin," *British Journal of Canadian Studies* 30, no. 2 (2018): 205–22; Braden Te Hiwi, "'Unlike Their Playmates of Civilization, the Indian Children's Recreation Must Be Cultivated and Developed': The Administration of Physical Education at Pelican Lake Indian Residential School, 1926–1944," *Historical Studies in Education/Revue d'histoire de l'education* 29, no. 1 (2017): 99–118; and Braden Te Hiwi and Janice Forsyth, "'A Rink at This School Is Almost as Essential as a Classroom': Hockey and Discipline at Pelican Lake Indian Residential School, 1945–1951," *Canadian Journal of History* 52, no. 1 (2017): 80–108.

Introduction: Picturing the Past

1 Quoted in Sarah de Leeuw, "'If Anything Is to Be Done with the Indian, We Must Catch Him Very Young': Colonial Constructions of Aboriginal Children and the Geographies of Indian Residential Schooling in British Columbia, Canada," *Children's Geographies* 7, no. 2 (2009): 131, https://doi.org/10.1080/14733280902798837.

2 Lucy Affleck to Graham, Commissioner of Indian Affairs, Regina, 15 November 1929, LAC, RG10, c-9810, Vol. 6332, file 661–1, part 2.

3 Affleck to Graham, 15 November 1929, LAC.

4 A.G. Hamilton, Inspector's Report: Birtle Residential School, 4 December 1936, LAC, RG 10, c-13800, Volume 8449, file 511/23-5-014.

5 Arthur Bear Chief, *My Decade at Old Sun, My Lifetime of Hell*, Our Lives: Diary, Memoir, and Letters Imprint (Edmonton: AU Press, 2016), 25.

6 Sigrid Lien and Hilde Nielssen, "Absence and Presence: The Work of Photographs in the Sámi Museum, RiddoDuottarMuseat-Sámiid Vuorká-Dávvirat (RDM-SVD) in Karasjok, Norway," *Photography and Culture* 5, no. 3 (2012): 303, https://doi.org/10.2752/175145212X13415789392965.

7 Kristen Dobbin, "'Exposing Yourself a Second Time': Visual Repatriation in Scandinavian Sápmi," *Visual Communication Quarterly* 20, no. 3 (2013): 141, https://doi.org/10.1080/15551393.2013.820585.

8 Veli-Pekka Lehtola, "Our Histories in the Photographs of the Others: Sámi Approaches to Visual Materials in Archives," *Journal of Aesthetics and Culture* 10, no. 4 (2018): 11, https://doi.org/10.1080/20004214.2018.1510647.

9 O.B. Strapp,? 1947, Brandon Residential School, 1946–47 [Yearbook].

10 An important point here is one famously made by Brownlie and Kelm: that the demonstrable resiliency of those experiencing oppression does not excuse the profoundly damaging impacts of government agents and missionaries. Robin Brownlie and Mary-Ellen Kelm, "Desperately Seeking Absolution: Native Agency as Colonialist Alibi?" *Canadian Historical Review* 75, no. 4 (1994): 543–56.

11 Nishnawbe Aski Nation 35th-year Documentary, directed by Rabbithead, YouTube, 24 September 2012, https://youtu.be/jqD6c2gUM94.

Chapter 1: The Whole Story

1 Elizabeth Edwards, "Talking Visual Histories: Introduction," in *Museums and Source Communities: A Routledge Reader*, ed. Laura Peers and Alison K. Brown, 1st ed. (London: Routledge, 2003), 84.

2 Jane Lydon, "'Behold the Tears': Photography as Colonial Witness," *History of Photography* 34, no. 3 (2010): 247, https://doi.org/10.1080/03087291003765836.

3 Examples include Ann Fienup-Riordan, *The Living Tradition of Yup'ik Masks: Agayuliyararput; Our Way of Making Prayer*, 1st ed. (Seattle: University of Washington Press, 1996); Joshua A. Bell, "Looking to See: Reflections on Visual Repatriation in the Purari Delta, Gulf Province, Papua New Guinea," in *Museums and Source Communities: A Routledge Reader*, ed. Laura Peers and Alison K Brown, 1st ed. (London: Routledge, 2003), 111–22.

4 Alison K. Brown, Laura L. Peers, and Members of the Kainai Nation, *Pictures Bring Us Messages / Sinaakssiiksi Aohtsimaahpihkookiyaawa: Photographs and Histories from the Kainai Nation* (Toronto: University of Toronto Press, 2006).

5 Celeste Pedri-Spade, "Waasaabikizo: Our Pictures Are Good Medicine," *Decolonization: Indigeneity, Education and Society* 5, no. 1 (2016): 45–70.

6 Jane Lydon, "Return: The Photographic Archive and Technologies of Indigenous Memory," *Photographies* 3, no. 2 (2010): 179.

7 Lydon, "Behold the Tears," 247.

8 Carol Payne, "A Land of Youth: Nationhood and the Image of the Child in the National Film Board of Canada's Still Photography Division," in *Depicting Canada's Children*, ed. Loren R. Lerner (Waterloo: Wilfrid Laurier University Press, 2009), 85–107.

9 Payne, "Land of Youth," 90.

10 Carol Payne, *The Official Picture: The National Film Board of Canada's Still Photography Division and the Image of Canada, 1941–1971*, McGill-Queen's-Beaverbrook Canadian Foundation Studies in Art History (Montréal: McGill-Queen's University Press, 2013), 7.

11 Payne, *Official Picture*, 12.

12 Gar Lunney, "Interview by Charity Marple," 7 May 1996, Canadian Museum of Contemporary Photography, NFB SPD collection, National Gallery of Canada, 1996.

13 Braden Te Hiwi and Janice Forsyth, "'A Rink at This School Is Almost as Essential as a Classroom': Hockey and Discipline at Pelican Lake Indian Residential School, 1945–1951," *Canadian Journal of History* 52, no. 1 (2017): 80–108.

14 Adele Stalmach, "Native Women and Work: Changing Representations in Photographs from the Collections of the National Film Board and of the Department of Indian Affairs and Northern Development" (Master's thesis, Carleton University, 1995); Carol Payne, *The Official Picture*, 14.

15 Richard S. Gruneau and David Whitson, *Hockey Night in Canada: Sport, Identities, and Cultural Politics*, Culture and Communication in Canada Series (Toronto: Garamond Press, 1993); Carly Adams and Jason Laurendeau, "'Here They Come! Look Them Over!': Youth, Citizenship, and the Emergence of Minor Hockey in Canada," in *Hockey: Challenging Canada's Game—Au-delà du sport national*, ed. Jenny Ellison and Jennifer Anderson (Ottawa: University of Ottawa Press, 2018), 121.

16 Braden Paora Te Hiwi, "Physical Culture as Citizenship Education at Pelican Lake Indian Residential School, 1926–1970" (PhD diss., University of Western Ontario, 2015).

17 Fatima Ba'abbad, "History of Sioux Lookout Black Hawks Hockey Team, 1949–1951" (Master's thesis, University of Western Ontario, 2017), 61.

18 David Bruce MacDonald, *The Sleeping Giant Awakens: Genocide, Indian Residential Schools, and the Challenge of Conciliation* (Toronto: University of Toronto Press, 2019), 14.

19 TRC, *Canada's Residential Schools: The History, Part 1, Origins to 1939* (Montreal and Kingston: Truth and Reconciliation Commission of Canada, 2015), 16.

20 TRC, *Canada's Residential Schools: The History, Part 1*, 15.

21 TRC, *Canada's Residential Schools: The History, Part 1*, 17.

22 Sarah de Leeuw, "'If Anything Is to Be Done with the Indian, We Must Catch Him Very Young': Colonial Constructions of Aboriginal Children and the Geographies of Indian Residential Schooling in British Columbia, Canada," *Children's Geographies* 7, no. 2 (2009): 126, https://doi. org/10.1080/14733280902798837.

23 MacDonald, *The Sleeping Giant*, 16.

24 Pamela Palmater, "Genocide, Indian Policy, and Legislated Elimination of Indians in Canada," *Aboriginal Policy Studies* 3, no. 3 (2014), https://doi.org/10.5663/aps.v3i3.22225.

25 Sean Carleton, *Lessons in Legitimacy: Colonialism, Capitalism, and the Rise of State Schooling in British Columbia* (Vancouver: UBC Press, 2022).

26 Krista Maxwell, "Settler-Humanitarianism: Healing the Indigenous Child-Victim," *Comparative Studies in Society and History* 59, no. 4 (2017): 980, https://doi.org/10.1017/S0010417517000342.

27 Christina Firpo and Margaret Jacobs, "Taking Children, Ruling Colonies: Child Removal and Colonial Subjugation in Australia, Canada, French Indochina, and the United States, 1870–1950s," *Journal of World History* 29, no. 4 (2018): 531, https://doi.org/10.1353/jwh.2018.0054.

28 TRC, *They Came for the Children: Canada, Aboriginal Peoples, and Residential Schools* (Winnipeg: Truth and Reconciliation Commission of Canada, 2012), 5.

29 MacDonald, *The Sleeping Giant*; Maxwell, "Settler-Humanitarianism."

30 Maxwell, "Settler-Humanitarianism," 980.

31 MacDonald, *The Sleeping Giant*.

32 Andrew Armitage, *Comparing the Policy of Aboriginal Assimilation: Australia, Canada, and New Zealand* (Vancouver: UBC Press, 1998), 78.

33 Christine O'Bonsawin, "The Assertion of Canada's Colonial Self in National and International Sport," in *Sport and Recreation in Canadian History*, ed. Carly Adams, 1st ed. (Champaign: Human Kinetics Publishers, 2020), 282.

34 Armitage, *Policy of Aboriginal Assimilation*, 78.

35 O'Bonsawin, "The Assertion of Canada's Colonial Self."

36 Gar Lunney, "Interview by Charity Marple," 7 May 1996, Canadian Museum of Contemporary Photography, NFB SPD collection, National Gallery of Canada, 1996.

37 Stalmach, "Native Women and Work," 53.

38 Stalmach, "Native Women and Work," 52.

39 Bruce M. White, *We Are at Home: Pictures of the Ojibwe People* (St. Paul: Minnesota Historical Society Press, 2007), 14.

40 Jessica Ball and Pauline Janyst, "Enacting Research Ethics in Partnerships with Indigenous Communities in Canada: 'Do It in a Good Way,'" *Journal of Empirical Research on Human Research Ethics* 3, no. 2 (2008): 48, https://doi.org/10.1525/jer.2008.3.2.33.

41 Chelsea Bond, Murray G. Phillips, and Gary Osmond, "Crossing Lines: Sport History, Transformative Narratives, and Aboriginal Australia," *International Journal of the History of Sport* 32, no. 13 (2 September 2015): 1538, https://doi.org/10.1080/09523367.2015.1038704.

42 Survivors of the Assiniboia Indian Residential School and edited by Andrew Woolford, *Did You See Us? Reunion, Remembrance, and Reclamation at an Urban Indian Residential School* (Winnipeg: University of Manitoba Press, 2021).

43 Mary Jane Logan McCallum, *Nii Ndahlohke: Boys' and Girls' Work at Mount Elgin Industrial School, 1890–1915* (Altona, MB: FriesenPress, 2022).

44 "About," Manitoba Indigenous Tuberculosis History Project, University of Winnipeg, https://indigenoustbhistory.ca/about.

45 John Paul Lederach, *The Moral Imagination: The Art and Soul of Building Peace* (New York: Oxford University Press, 2005), 140.

46 Bond, Phillips, and Osmond, "Crossing Lines," 1539.

47 Jeff Corntassel, T'lakwadzi, and Chaw-win-is, "Indigenous Storytelling, Truth-Telling, and Community Approaches to Reconciliation," *ESC: English Studies in Canada* 35, no. 1 (2009): 137–59, https://doi.org/10.1353/esc.0.0163.

48 Robina Anne Thomas, "Honouring the Oral Traditions of My Ancestors through Storytelling—Qwul'sih'yah'maht," in *Research as Resistance: Critical, Indigenous and Anti-Oppressive Approaches*, ed. Leslie Brown and Susan Strega (Toronto: Canadian Scholars' Press, 2005), 241–42.

49 National Centre for Truth and Reconciliation (NCTR), "Dialogues: Nothing for us without us," 14 July 2020. Available online at https://www.youtube.com/watch?v=gYQFgvrvOzc.

50 Paulette Regan, *Unsettling the Settler Within: Indian Residential Schools, Truth Telling, and Reconciliation in Canada* (Vancouver: UBC Press, 2010), 78. Our incorporation of the works of Lederach and Longchari was inspired by Regan's engagement with their insights on restorying, peacebuilding, and reconciliation.

51 Lederach, *The Moral Imagination*, 146.

Chapter 2: The Truth About Photographs

1 Jeffrey Montez de Oca and José Prado, "Visualizing Humanitarian Colonialism: Photographs From the Thomas Indian School," *American Behavioral Scientist* 58, no. 1 (2014): 145–70, https://doi.org/10.1177/0002764213495027.

2 Joanna Cohan Scherer, "You Can't Believe Your Eyes: Inaccuracies in Photographs of North American Indians," *Studies in Visual Communications* 2, no. 2 (1975): 67–79, https://doi.org/10.1525/var.1975.2.2.67; Lee Clark Mitchell, "The Photograph and the American Indian," in *The Photograph and the American Indian*, ed. Alfred L. Bush and Lee Clark Mitchell (Princeton, NJ: Princeton University Press, 1994).

3 Mitchell, "The Photograph and the American Indian," xiii.

4 Anna Grimshaw, *The Ethnographer's Eye: Ways of Seeing in Anthropology* (Cambridge: Cambridge University Press, 2001), 4, https://doi.org/10.1017/CBO9780511817670.

5 John Bale, "Capturing 'The African' Body? Visual Images and 'Imaginative Sports,'" *Journal of Sport History* 25, no. 2 (1998): 235.

6 Bale, "Capturing 'The African' Body."

7 Lonna M. Malmsheimer, "'Imitation White Man': Images of Transformation at the Carlisle Indian School," *Studies in Visual Communication* 11, no. 4 (1985): 54–75, https://doi.org/10.1111/j.2326-8492.1985.tb00135.x; Carol Payne, "Through a Canadian Lens: Discourses of Nationalism and Aboriginal Representation in Governmental Photographs," in *Visual Communication and Culture: Images in Action*, ed. Jonathan M. Finn (Don Mills, Ontario: Oxford University Press, 2012), 310–25.

8 Brook Andrew and Jessica Neath, "Encounters with Legacy Images: Decolonising and Re-Imagining Photographic Evidence from the Colonial Archive," *History of Photography* 42, no. 3 (2018): 224, https://doi.org/10.1080/03087298.2018.1440933.
9 Alison K. Brown, Laura L. Peers, and Members of the Kainai Nation, *Pictures Bring Us Messages / Sinaakssiiksi Aohtsimaahpihkookiyaawa: Photographs and Histories from the Kainai Nation* (Toronto: University of Toronto Press, 2006).
10 Brown et al., *Pictures Bring Us Messages,* 34.
11 Bale, "Capturing the 'African' Body," 235.
12 Jane Lydon, "Behold the Tears: Photography as Colonial Witness," *History of Photography* 34, no. 3 (2010): 235.
13 Bale, "Capturing the 'African' Body," 236.
14 Grimshaw, *The Ethnographer's Eye.*
15 Grimshaw, *The Ethnographer's Eye*, 21–22.
16 Grimshaw, *The Ethnographer's Eye*, 23.
17 Kristen Dobbin, "'Exposing Yourself a Second Time': Visual Repatriation in Scandinavian Sápmi," *Visual Communication Quarterly* 20, no. 3 (2013): 132, https://doi.org/10.1080/15551393.2013.820585.
18 Dobbin, "Exposing Yourself a Second Time."
19 Grimshaw, *The Ethnographer's Eye.*
20 Brown et al., *Pictures Bring Us Messages.*
21 Marcus Banks and Richard Vokes, "Introduction: Anthropology, Photography and the Archive," *History and Anthropology* 21, no. 4 (2010): 337–49, https://doi.org/10.1080/02757206.2010.522375.
22 Andrew and Neath, "Encounters with Legacy Images," 225.
23 Scherer, "You Can't Believe Your Eyes," 67.
24 Scherer, "You Can't Believe Your Eyes," 67.
25 Scherer, "You Can't Believe Your Eyes."
26 Scherer, "You Can't Believe Your Eyes."
27 Daniel Francis, *The Imaginary Indian: The Image of the Indian in Canadian Culture* (Vancouver: Arsenal Pulp Press, 1992), 56.
28 Brown et al., *Pictures Bring Us Messages*, 35.
29 Scherer, "You Can't Believe Your Eyes," 77.
30 Brown et al., *Pictures Bring Us Messages,* 34.
31 Francis, *Imaginary Indian*, 53.
32 Brown et al., *Pictures Bring Us Messages*, 34.
33 Payne, "Through a Canadian Lens."
34 Banks and Vokes, "Introduction: Anthropology, Photography and the Archive," 343.
35 Carol Payne, "Lessons with Leah: Re-reading the Photographic Archive of Nation in the National Film Board of Canada's Still Photography Division," *Visual Studies* 21, no. 1 (2006): 4–22, https://doi.org/10.1080/14725860600613147.
36 Payne, "Lessons with Leah."
37 Payne, "Through a Canadian Lens."

38 Philip J. Hatfield, *Canada in the Frame: Copyright, Collections and the Image of Canada, 1895–1924* (London: UCL Press, 2018), 88–89.

39 Hatfield, *Canada in the Frame*, 90.

40 Hatfield, *Canada in the Frame*, 89.

41 Martel and Sons, *Illustrated Souvenir of Brandon, Manitoba*, W. Warner: Brandon, Manitoba, 1909?; No author.

42 Alexandra Giancarlo, "Indigenous Student Labour and Settler Colonialism at Brandon Residential School," *Canadian Geographies* 64, no. 3 (2020): 461–74, https://doi.org/10.1111/cag.12613.

43 W.G. MacFarlane, *Photographic View Album of Brandon, Manitoba* (Brandon, MB: D.E. Clement, c. 1901).

44 Bruce Alden Cox, "Historical Anthropology," in *A Different Drummer: Readings in Anthropology with a Canadian Perspective*, ed. Bruce Alden Cox, Jacques Chevalier, and Valda Blundell (Montreal: McGill-Queen's University Press, 1987), 34, https://doi.org/10.1515/9780773595804.

45 Cox, "Historical Anthropology"; Jan Penrose, "When All the Cowboys Are Indians: The Nature of Race in All-Indian Rodeo," *Annals of the Association of American Geographers* 93, no. 3 (2003): 687–705, https://doi.org/10.1111/1467-8306.9303009.

46 Cited in Cox, "Historical Anthropology," 35.

47 "Hudson Bay Railroad: The Surveying Staff Organized for Work," *Globe*, May 6, 1895.

48 Marianne Hirsch and Leo Spitzer, *School Photos in Liquid Time: Reframing Difference* (Seattle: University of Washington Press, 2020), 71.

49 Hirsch and Spitzer, *School Photos*, 61.

50 Hirsch and Spitzer, *School Photos*.

51 Lonna M. Malmsheimer, "'Imitation White Man': Images of Transformation at the Carlisle Indian School," *Studies in Visual Communication* 11, no. 4 (1985): 54–75.

52 Naomi Angel and Pauline Wakeham, "Witnessing *In Camera*: Photographic Reflections on Truth and Reconciliation," in *Arts of Engagement: Taking Aesthetic Action in and Beyond the Truth and Reconciliation Commission of Canada*, ed. Dylan Robinson and Keavy Martin (Waterloo: Wilfrid Laurier University Press, 2016), 93–134, https://doi.org/10.51644/9781771121705-006; Miranda J. Brady and Emily Hiltz, "The Archaeology of an Image: The Persistent Persuasion of Thomas Moore Keesick's Residential School Photographs," *TOPIA: Canadian Journal of Cultural Studies* 37 (2017): 61–85, https://doi.org/10.3138/topia.37.61.

53 Jeffrey Montez de Oca and José Prado, "Visualizing Humanitarian Colonialism: Photographs From the Thomas Indian School," *American Behavioral Scientist* 58, no. 1 (2014): 145, https://doi.org/10.1177/0002764213495027.

54 Nicole Strathman, "Student Snapshots: An Alternative Approach to the Visual History of American Indian Boarding Schools," *Humanities* 4, no. 4 (2015): 726–47, https://doi.org/10.3390/h4040726; Eric Margolis, "Looking at Discipline, Looking at Labour: Photographic Representations of Indian Boarding Schools," *Visual Studies* 19, no. 1 (2004): 72–96, https://doi.org/10.1080/1472586042000204861.

55 Eric Margolis and Jeremy Rowe, "Images of Assimilation: Photographs of Indian Schools in Arizona," *History of Education* 33, no. 2 (2004): 199–230, https://doi.org/10.1080/0046760032000151456.

56 Malmsheimer, "'Imitation White Man,'" 57.

57 John Chi-Kit Wong, "Proem," in *Coast to Coast: Hockey in Canada to the Second World War*, ed. John Chi-Kit Wong (Buffalo: University of Toronto Press, 2009), x.

58 Wong, "Proem."

59 Carly Adams and Jason Laurendeau, "'Here They Come! Look Them over!': Youth, Citizenship, and the Emergence of Minor Hockey in Canada," in *Hockey: Challenging Canada's Game—Au-delà du sport national*, ed. Jenny Ellison and Jennifer Anderson (Ottawa: University of Ottawa Press, 2018), 120, https://doi.org/10.2307/j.ctt22rbkfw.

60 Quote from the 1953 National Film Board documentary, *Here's Hockey!* in Andrew Holman, "A Flag of Tendons: Hockey and Canadian History," in *Hockey: Challenging Canada's Game—Au-delà du sport national*, ed. by Jenny Ellison and Jennifer Anderson (Ottawa: University of Ottawa Press, 2018), 35, https://doi.org/10.2307/j.ctt22rbkfw.

Chapter 3: Promoting the "Good Work" of Schooling

1 J.P.B. Ostrander, Regional Supervisor of Indian Agencies, Saskatchewan, to Indian Affairs Branch, Department of Mines and Resources, Ottawa, 12 June 1948, LAC, RG 10, c-9807, Volume 6327, File 660-1, Part 3.

2 Jean Barman, "Sports and the Development of Character," in *Sports in Canada*, ed. Morris Mott (Mississauga, ON: Copp Clark Pitman, 1989), 242; Norman Knowles, "'By the Mouth of Many Messengers': Mission and Social Service in Canadian Anglicanism (1867–1945)," in *Seeds Scattered and Sown: Studies in the History of Canadian Anglicanism*, ed. N. Knowles (Toronto: ABC Publishing, 2008), 174.

3 "An Outline of the Duties of Those Who Occupy Positions on the Staff at the Society's Indian Residential Schools, No. III, The Teacher," n.d., GS, 75-103, Box 131, File 5, Indian and Eskimo Residential School Commission.

4 Department of Indian Affairs, *Daily Register for Recording the Attendance of Indian School Pupils* (Ottawa: Government Printing Bureau, 1927).

5 Department of Indian Affairs, *Calisthenics and Games, Prepared for Use in All Indian Schools* (Ottawa: Government Printing Bureau, 1910), 17.

6 Celia Haig-Brown, Garry Gottfriedson, Randy Fred, and the KIRS Survivors, *Tsqelmucwilc: The Kamloops Indian Residential School—Resistance and a Reckoning* (Vancouver: Arsenal Pulp Press, 2022), 126.

7 Rev. M. Bretagne, Principal of Lebret Indian Industrial School, to R.A. Hoey, Supt. Welfare and Training, Indian Affairs Branch, Ottawa, 27 May 1939, LAC, RG 10, c-9807, Volume 6327, File 660-1, Part 3.

8 John Bloom, "'There Is Madness in the Air': The 1926 Haskell Homecoming and Popular Representations of Sports in Federal Indian Boarding Schools," in *Dressing in Feathers: The Construction of the Indian in American Popular Culture*, ed. S.E. Bird (Boulder: Routledge, 1996), 102–109.

9 William Medina, "Selling Indians at Sherman Institute, 1902–1922" (PhD diss., University of California, Riverside, 2007), 74–108.

10 Janice Forsyth, "The Indian Act and the (Re)Shaping of Canadian Aboriginal Sport Practices," *International Journal of Canadian Studies*, no. 35 (2007): 95–111, https://doi.org/10.7202/040765ar; J.R. Miller, *Shingwauk's Vision: A History of Native Residential Schools* (Toronto: University of Toronto Press, 1996).

11 T. Ferrier, Superintendent of Methodist Indian Schools and Hospitals in Canada, to the Superintendent of Indian Affairs, Ottawa, 11 December 1923, LAC School Files Series, RG 10, Volume 6255, File 576-1, part 2.

12 Jean Telfer, "The Indian Residential School," [1931–1940]. Item 009. Jean Telfer Fonds, the Museum of Anthropology, the University of British Columbia.

13 Miller, *Shingwauk's Vision*, 217–18.

14 J.R. Naessens, "Annual Report on High River Industrial School," in *Annual Report of the Department of Indian Affairs, for the year ending June 30, 1899* (Ottawa: Department of Indian Affairs, 1900).

15 J.R. Motion, "Annual Report on Alberni Boarding School," in *Annual Report of the Department of Indian Affairs, for the fiscal year ended 30th June 1904* (Ottawa: Department of Indian Affairs, 1905).

16 *National Monthly of Canada*, Volume 3, no. 5 (November 1903).

17 *National Monthly of Canada*, Volume 3, no. 5 (November 1903).

18 Forsyth, "The Indian Act"; Janice Forsyth, "The Power to Define: A History of the Tom Longboat Awards, 1951–2001" (PhD diss., University of Western Ontario, 2005).

19 Janice Forsyth, *Reclaiming Tom Longboat: Indigenous Self-Determination in Canadian Sport* (Regina: University of Regina Press, 2020), 47.

20 Forsyth, *Reclaiming Tom Longboat*, 47–48.

21 Forsyth, *Reclaiming Tom Longboat*, 48.

22 Heidi Bohaker and Franca Iacovetta, "Making Aboriginal People 'Immigrants Too': A Comparison of Citizenship Programs for Newcomers and Indigenous Peoples in Postwar Canada, 1940s–1960s," *Canadian Historical Review* 90, no. 3 (2009): 427–62, https://doi.org/10.3138/chr.90.3.427.

23 Bohaker and Iacovetta, "Making Aboriginal People 'Immigrants Too,'" 428–29.

24 We specify that this distinctiveness is superficial, because the boys did not play lacrosse as part of their culture. However, the lacrosse stick—like the totem pole—was an easily recognizable "Indigenous" symbol by white Canadians.

25 Bohaker and Iacovetta, "Making Aboriginal People 'Immigrants Too,'" 436.

26 TRC, *Canada's Residential Schools: The History, Part 2, 1939 to 2000* (Montreal and Kingston: Truth and Reconciliation Commission of Canada, 2015), 18.

27 Bohaker and Iacovetta, "Making Aboriginal People 'Immigrants Too.'"

28 Forsyth, "The Indian Act."

29 Canada, *Report of Indian Affairs Branch for the Fiscal Year Ended March 21, 1953* (Ottawa: Department of Citizenship and Immigration, 1953), Library and Archives Canada, Indian Affairs Annual Reports, 1864–1990; Canada, *Report of Indian Affairs*

Branch for the Fiscal Year Ended March 31, 1954 (Ottawa: Department of Citizenship and Immigration, 1954), Library and Archives Canada, Indian Affairs Annual Reports, 1864–1990.

30 "Sault Agrees to Assist Garden River Sports Plan." *Sault Daily Star*, 4 July 1951, 14, private collection.

31 "Sault Agrees to Assist Garden River Sports Plan."

32 Department of Citizenship and Immigration, Indian Affairs Branch, Education Division, *Indian School Bulletin*, May 1950, 14.

33 Department of Citizenship and Immigration, Indian Affairs Branch, Education Division, *Indian School Bulletin*, May 1950, 16.

34 Department of Citizenship and Immigration, Indian Affairs Branch, Education Division, *Indian School Bulletin*, May 1950, 16.

35 Amy Von Heyking, *Creating Citizens: History and Identity in Alberta's Schools, 1905–1980* (Calgary: University of Calgary Press, 2006).

36 Department of Citizenship and Immigration, Indian Affairs Branch, Education Division, *Indian School Bulletin*, November 1951, 10.

37 R.D. Ragan, Regional Supervisor of Indian Agencies, to Mr. R.F. Davey, Superintendent of Education, Re: Brandon Indian Residential School, 8 February 1957, LAC School Files Series, RG 10, Volume 7194, File 511/25-1-015.

38 Harry Atkinson [temporary principal at Brandon Residential School] to Rev. G. McMillan, United Church of Canada, Re—Our conversation over the phone—April 15th, 17 April 1957. United Church of Canada Archives MNWO/ANCC, Winnipeg, MB.

39 Jeffrey Montez de Oca and Jose Prado, "Visualizing Humanitarian Colonialism: Photographs from the Thomas Indian School," *American Behavioral Scientist* 58, no. 1 (2014): 145.

40 Christopher J. Greig, *Ontario Boys: Masculinity and the Idea of Boyhood in Postwar Ontario, 1945–1960* (Waterloo: Wilfrid Laurier University Press, 2014).

41 Greig, *Ontario Boys*, xii.

42 Cynthia R. Comacchio, *The Dominion of Youth: Adolescence and the Making of a Modern Canada, 1920–1950* (Waterloo: Wilfrid Laurier University Press, 2006), 191.

43 Krista McCracken, "Archival Photographs in Perspective: Indian Residential School Images of Health," *British Journal of Canadian Studies* 30, no. 2 (2017): 173.

44 Taylor McKee and Janice Forsyth, "Witnessing Painful Pasts: Understanding Images of Sports at Canadian Indian Residential Schools," *Journal of Sport History* 46, no. 2 (2019): 175–88.

45 John Bloom, "The Imperial Gridiron: Dealing with the Legacy of Carlisle Indian School Sports," in *Carlisle Indian Industrial School: Indigenous Histories, Memories, and Reclamations*, ed. Jacqueline Fear-Segal and Susan D. Rose (Lincoln: University of Nebraska Press, 2016), 124.

46 McKee and Forsyth, "Witnessing Painful Pasts," 177.

Chapter 4: Surviving Pelican Lake

1 John Sheridan Milloy, *A National Crime: The Canadian Government and the Residential School System, 1879 to 1986* (Winnipeg: University of Manitoba Press, 2017), 205.

2 Grant Charles and Mike DeGagné, "Student-to-Student Abuse in the Indian Residential Schools in Canada: Setting the Stage for Further Understanding," *Child and Youth Services* 34, no. 4 (2013): 346, https://doi.org/10.1080/0145935X.2013.859903.

3 Cited in Milloy, *A National Crime*, 191.

4 Cited in Braden Paora Te Hiwi, "Physical Culture as Citizenship Education at Pelican Lake Indian Residential School, 1926–1970" (PhD diss., University of Western Ontario, 2015), 139.

5 Te Hiwi, "Physical Culture as Citizenship Education"; Milloy, *A National Crime*, 226–27.

6 Mary Jane Logan McCallum, *Nii Ndahlohke: Boys' and Girls' Work at Mount Elgin Industrial School, 1890–1915* (Altona, MB: FriesenPress, 2022), 29.

7 "The Sioux Lookout School," n.d., General Synod Archives of the Anglican Church (GS), 75-103, Box 131, File 4, The Indian and Eskimo Residential School Commission of the MSCC (IERSC).

8 Mary Jane Logan McCallum, *Indigenous Women, Work, and History, 1940–1980* (Winnipeg: University of Manitoba Press, 2014).

9 "The Sioux Lookout School," n.d., GS, 75-103, Box 131, File 4, The Indian and Eskimo Residential School Commission of the MSCC (IERSC).

10 "The Sioux Lookout School," n.d., GS, 75-103, Box 131, File 4, The Indian and Eskimo Residential School Commission of the MSCC (IERSC).

11 "The Sioux Lookout School," n.d., GS, 75-103, Box 131, File 4, The Indian and Eskimo Residential School Commission of the MSCC (IERSC).

12 G. Swartman, Agent's Report for the Quarter Ending December 31st, 1945, LAC, RG 10, c-7948, Volume 6220, File 472-5, Part 6.

13 "The Survivors Speak: A Report of the Truth and Reconciliation Commission of Canada" (Truth and Reconciliation Commission of Canada, 2015), 82.

14 C.A. Clark, Educational Survey Officer, Department of Citizenship and Immigration, Indian Affairs Canada, to Superintendent of Education, 20 October 1951, LAC, RG 10, c-9717, Volume 8797, File 1/25-13-1, Part 1.

15 G. Swartman, Re: Sioux Lookout Indian Residential School, 28 January 1952, LAC, RG 10, c-13764, Volume 8274, File 494/6-1-014, Part 1.

16 "Remembering the Bad Old Days in the Residential School," 1972. Archived episode of CBC radio program *Our Native Land*, hosted by Johnny Yesno [former Black Hawk]. Available at https://www.cbc.ca/player/play/1402943356.

17 "Sioux Youngsters Seek Jobs, Hockey Careers at Lakehead," *Port Arthur News-Chronicle*, 18 November 1953.

18 C.A. Clark, Educational Survey Officer, Department of Citizenship and Immigration, Indian Affairs Canada, to Superintendent of Education, 29 October 1951, LAC, RG 10, c-9717, Volume 8797, File 1/25-13-1, Part 1.

19 H.G. Mingay, Regional Inspector of Indian Schools, "Enquiry re Shingwauk and Sioux Lookout Residential Schools," 1951, LAC, c-9717, Volume 8797, File 1/25-13-1, Part 1.

20 Philip Phelan to Mr. G. Swartman, Superintendent, Indian Agency, Sioux Lookout, Ontario, 21 November 1952, LAC, RG 10, c-13764, Volume 8274, File 494/6-0-014, Part 1.

21 "Remembering the Bad Old Days," 1972.

22 R.D. Gidney, *From Hope to Harris: The Reshaping of Ontario's Schools* (Toronto: University of Toronto Press, 2002), 11–12.

23 G. Swartman, Agent's Report for the Quarter Ending December 31st, 1945, LAC, RG 10, c-7948, Volume 6220, File 472-5, Part 6.

24 Extract from Quarterly Report for the Period Ended December 31st, 1952, re: Sioux Lookout Indian Agency, LAC, RG 10, c-13764, Volume 8274, File 494/6-0-014, Part 2.

25 K.S. Evans, A. Lindsay, and N.J. Sinclair, "Forced to Work 'Too Hard': A Case Study of Forced Child Labour and Slavery in Manitoba's Indian Residential Schools," *At The Forks* 1, no. 1 (2023), https://ojs.lib.umanitoba.ca/index.php/forks/article/view/921; Alexandra Giancarlo, "Indigenous Student Labour and Settler Colonialism at Brandon Residential School," *The Canadian Geographer* 63, no. 3 (2020): 461–74.

26 "The Sioux Lookout School," n.d., GS, 75-103, Box 131, File 4, The Indian and Eskimo Residential School Commission of the MSCC (IERSC).

27 Te Hiwi, "Physical Culture as Citizenship Education," 57, 64.

28 Brandon Indian Residential School, 1943–44 [Yearbook], no author.

29 Robert P. Wells, *Wawahte: Indian Residential Schools* (Victoria, BC: FriesenPress, 2016).

30 Te Hiwi, "Physical Culture as Citizenship Education," 103.

31 Quoted in Te Hiwi, "Physical Culture as Citizenship Education," 65.

32 Te Hiwi, "Physical Culture as Citizenship Education," 64.

33 Department of Indian Affairs, *Calisthenics and Games, Prepared for Use in All Indian Schools* (Ottawa: Government Printing Bureau, 1910), 3.

34 Clare Sheridan (presumed), 1930s, c. [1931–1940], handwritten notes from what would become *Redskin Interlude*. Jean Telfer Fonds, Museum of Anthropology, University of British Columbia (item 0130). Vancouver, British Columbia, Canada.

35 T.B.R. Westgate to the Secretary at the Department of Indian Affairs, 7 July 1927, LAC, RG 10, Volume 6215, File 470-5, Part 1.

36 Rev. J. Marshall to the Secretary at the Department of Indian Affairs, August 15, 1930, LAC, RG 10, Volume 6215, File 470-5, Part 2.

37 Henry G. Cook to Colonel Neary, Superintendent of Indian Education, 26 June 1950, LAC, RG 10, c-13764, Volume 8274, File 494/6–1-014, Part 1.

38 G. Swartman, Quarterly Report Ending March 1945, on Sioux Lookout Agency, LAC, RG 10, Volume 6216, File 470–5, Part 6.

39 Missionary Society of the Church of England in Canada, *The Canadian Indian: Our Responsibility and Opportunity*, November 1945, GS 75–103, Box 131, File 1.

40 M.G. Webster, "Report of Visit of Miss M.G. Webster to Chapleau, Elkhorn, and Sioux Lookout Schools," 29 March–8 April 1947, GS 75–103, Box 23, File 4; "Report of Superintendent on Visit to Sioux Lookout," 15 March 1947, GS 75–103, Box 23, File 4.

41 G. Swartman to Indian Affairs Branch, 19 July 1951, LAC, RG 10, Volume 8274, File 494/6–1-014, Part 1.

42 "The Sioux Lookout School," n.d., GS 75–103, Box 131, File 4, The Indian and Eskimo Residential School Commission of the MSCC (IERSC).

43 Memorandum of an Inquiry to the Cause and Circumstances of the Death of (N. N.), 7 January 1938, LAC, RG 10, Volume 6216, File 470-23, Part 1.

44 Extract from Report of J. M. Ridge to Dr. Moore, 1 October 1945, LAC, RG 10, Volume 6216, File 470-5, Part 6.

45 G.R. Turner, Special Memo, Re: Sioux Lookout Indian Residential School, 18–19 October 1948, GS 75–103, Box 23, File 5.

46 G. Swartman to Indian Affairs Branch, Department of Mines and Resources, 11 March 1949, LAC, c-7945, p. 1668, Volume 6216, File 470-23, Part 1.

47 W.M. Benedickson, M.P. for Kenora-Rainy River, to Colin Gibson, Minister of Mines and Resources, 21 September 1949, LAC, RG 10, c-7945, Volume 6216, File 470-5, Part 9.

48 G. Swartman to Indian Affairs Branch, Ottawa, Ontario, 10 September 1949, LAC, RG10, c-7945, Volume 6216, File 470-5, Part 9.

49 Philip Phelan to Mr. G. Swartman, Superintendent, Indian Agency, Sioux Lookout, Ontario, 26 September 1949, c-7945, Volume 6216, File 470-5, Part 9.

50 G.L. Bell to W.J. Wood, Medical Supt., Indian Health Services, Dominion Public Bldg., Winnipeg, MB, 30 September 1949, LAC c-7945, Volume 6216, File 470-5, Part 9.

51 G.R. Turner to Colonel B.F. Neary, Supt. of Indian Education, Indian Affairs Branch, Dept. of Mines and Resources, Ottawa, Ontario, 2 December 1949, LAC, c-7945, Volume 6216, File 470-5, Part 10.

52 Henry G. Cook to Colonel B.F. Neary, Supt. of Indian Education, Indian Affairs Branch, Dept. of Mines and Resources, Ottawa, Ontario, 3 February 1950, LAC, c-7945, Volume 6216, File 470-5, Part 10.

53 Letter from unknown writer to R.A. Gibson, Esq., Director, Development Services Branch, Department of Resources and Development, Norlite Building, Ottawa, Ontario, 1 May 1950, c-7945, Volume 6216, File 470-5, Part 10.

54 Indian Work Investigation Commission, *Report to the General Synod* (Winnipeg, 1946).

55 Henry G. Cook re: Indian Administration Schools, 7 February 1951, GS 75-103, Box 25, File 6.

56 Henry G. Cook to Philip Phelan, Superintendent of Education, Indian Affairs Branch, 24 November 1951, LAC, RG 10, Volume 8274, File 494/6–1-014, Part 1.

57 S.O. Barker, memorandum to Mr. Matters Re: Sioux Lookout I.R. School, 1953, LAC, RG 10, Volume 8274, File 494/6–1-014, Part 2.

58 Wells, *Wawahte*.

59 National Centre for Truth and Reconciliation (NTCR), "Pelican Lake (Pelican Falls)," https://nctr.ca/residential-schools/ontario/pelican-lake-pelican-falls/.

60 "The Survivors Speak: A Report of the Truth and Reconciliation Commission of Canada" (Truth and Reconciliation Commission of Canada, 2015), 177.

61 C.A. Clark, Educational Survey Officer, Department of Citizenship and Immigration, Indian Affairs Canada, to Superintendent of Education, 20 October 1951, LAC, RG 10, c-9717, Volume 8797, File 1/25-13-1, Part 1.

62 B.F. Neary, Superintendent of Welfare and Training, to Director, 5 December 1946, LAC, RG 10, c-8149, Volume 6033, File 150-44, Part 2.

63 Adam J. Barker, Toby Rollo, and Emma Battell Lowman, "Settler Colonialism and the Consolidation of Canada in the Twentieth Century," in *The Routledge Handbook of the History of Settler Colonialism*, ed. Edward Cavanagh and Lorenzo Veracini, 153–68 (Abingdon: Routledge, 2017), 163.

64 G.R. Turner, Visit of Superintendent to Sioux Lookout School, 31 May–2 June 1951, GS 75–103, Box 23, File 8.

65 Wells, *Wawahte*.

Chapter 5: Hockey Will Make Things Better

1 Henry G. Cook to Reverend J.N. Evans, 21 October 1948, GS 75–103, Box 23, File 5.

2 A. Routly, Superintendent's Visit to Sioux Lookout, 7–8 November 1948, GS 75–103, Box 23, File 5.

3 A. Routly, Superintendent's Visit to Sioux Lookout, 7–8 November 1948, GS 75–103, Box 23, File 5.

4 Henry G. Cook to P. Phelan, Re: Sport and Recreation, 5 June 1951, LAC, RG 10, Volume 8274, File 494/6–1-014, Part 1.

5 G. Swartman to Indian Affairs Branch, 19 July 1951, LAC, RG 10, Volume 8274, File 494/6–1-014, Part 1.

6 "Famous All-Indian Hockey Team Hawks Idea of Ex-Bush Pilots," 17 February 1951, *The News-Chronicle*, Sioux Lookout Community Museum (SLCM), Scrapbook of Gifford Swartman (henceforth, Swartman Scrapbook), "Black Hawks 1950/51."

7 Superintendent's Visit to Sioux Lookout, 28 January 1949, GS 75–103, Box 23, File 6.

8 SLCM, Swartman Scrapbook, "Black Hawks 1950/51."

9 SLCM, Swartman Scrapbook, "Black Hawks 1950/51."

10 J.R. Miller, *Shingwauk's Vision: A History of Native Residential Schools* (Toronto: University of Toronto Press, 1996), 275.

11 SLCM, Swartman Scrapbook, "Black Hawks 1950/51."

12 SLCM, Swartman Scrapbook, "Black Hawks 1950/51."

13 SLCM, Swartman Scrapbook, "Black Hawks 1950/51."

14 *Indian School Bulletin*, 4.4 (1950), Indian Affairs Branch, Indian and Northern Affairs Departmental Library, Rare Books Collection.

15 SLCM, Swartman Scrapbook, "Black Hawks 1950/51."

16 Jan Eisenhardt to F. Matters, 2 June 1950, Eisenhardt Collection, Weldon Library, Western University, Box 6, Folder 13, File 13.1, Item 6.

17 Bernard F. Neary to Mr. F. Matters, Regional Supervisor of Indian Agencies, Re: Sioux Lookout Indian Residential School, 1 March 1950, LAC, RG 10, C-7945, Volume 6216, File 470-5, Part 10.

18 Jan Eisenhardt to F. Matters, 2 June 1950, Eisenhardt Collection, Weldon Library, Western University, Box 6, Folder 13, File 13.1, Item 6.

19 SLCM, Swartman Scrapbook, "Black Hawks 1950/51."

20 Visit of Superintendent to Sioux Lookout School, 4 April 1950, GS 75–103, Box 23, File 7.

21 Visit of Superintendent to Sioux Lookout School.

22 "Twelve Indian Puck-Toters Here for Bantam Series," *Ottawa Evening Citizen*, 12 April 1951, 20.

23 "Twelve Indian Puck-Toters," 20.

24 "Bush-to-Bank-Street Leaves Boys Bug-Eyed," *Ottawa Journal*, 12 April 1951.

25 Department of Citizenship and Immigration, Indian Affairs Branch, Education Division, *Indian School Bulletin*, 1947, February 10. No. 3, Volume 1.

26 "Programme and Time Table in Connection with Ice Hockey Matches between the 'Black Hawks' Bantam Team from Sioux Lookout Indian Residential School and Ottawa Playground Team," EC, Box 6, Folder 12, File 12.1, Item 1, 1951?

27 "Indian Youngsters Being Royally Treated on Tour," *Saskatoon Star-Phoenix*, April 1951, SLCM, Swartman Scrapbook, "Black Hawks 1950/51."

28 "Indian Youngsters Being Royally Treated on Tour."

29 "Indians Impress with Hockey Prowess," SLCM, Swartman Scrapbook, "Black Hawks 1950/51."

30 Wilf Bell, "All-Indians Beat Ottawa East Six," *Ottawa Evening Citizen*, 14 April 1951, 22.

31 "Indian Youngsters Being Royally Treated on Tour."

32 Jack Kinsella, "Twelve Little Indians Take Ottawa by Storm During Peaceful Foray," *Hockey News*, 28 April 1951, SLCM, Swartman Scrapbook, "Black Hawks 1950/51."

33 "4-Foot Brave Wows 'Em," *Telegram*, 17 April 1951, SLCM, Swartman Scrapbook, "Black Hawks 1950/51."

34 Bob Fulford, "Indian Lads' Hockey Tour Cost $1,800—'Well Worth It,'" SLCM, Swartman Scrapbook, "Black Hawks 1950/51."

35 A. Narraway, "Settler Colonial Power and Indigenous Survival: Hockey Programs at Three Indian Residential Schools in Northwestern Ontario and Manitoba, 1929–1969" (PhD diss., Carleton University, 2018), 70, https://doi.org/10.22215/etd/2018-12887.

36 "Programme and Time Table."

37 "Programme and Time Table."

38 "Premier Plays Host to Indian Boys," SLCM, Swartman Scrapbook, "Black Hawks 1950/51."

39 Stan Houson, "All-Indian Team on Ice Warpath: Bantams from Sioux Lookout on Lookout for Scalps," *Telegram*, n.d., EC, Box 6, Folder 12, File 12.1, Item 4.

40 Fulford, "Indian Lads' Hockey Tour Cost $1,800—'Well Worth It.'"

41 Braden Paora Te Hiwi, "Physical Culture as Citizenship Education at Pelican Lake Indian Residential School, 1926-1970" (PhD diss., University of Western Ontario, 2015).

42 "Sioux Lookout Hawks Thrilled by Rendezvous," 4 July 1951, SLCM, Swartman Scrapbook, "Black Hawks 1950/51."

43 Braden Te Hiwi and Janice Forsyth, "'A Rink at This School Is Almost as Essential as a Classroom': Hockey and Discipline at Pelican Lake Indian Residential School, 1945–1951," *Canadian Journal of History* 52, no. 1 (2017): 80–108, https://doi.org/10.3138/cjh.ach.52.1.04.

44 G.R. Turner, Visit of Superintendent to Sioux Lookout School, 31 May–2 June 1951, GS 75–103, Box 23, File 8.

45 G. Swartman to Indian Affairs Branch, 19 July 1951, LAC, RG 10, Volume 8274, File 494/6–1-014, Part 1.

46 G.H. Marcoux, Regional Inspector for Indian Schools of Manitoba, to D.M. MacKay, Director, Indian Affairs Branch, Department of Citizenship and Immigration, Ottawa, Ontario, 9 August 1951, LAC School Files Series, RG 10, Volume 7194, File 511/25-01-15.

47 R.D. Ragan, Regional Supervisor of Indian Agencies, to Mr. R.F. Davey, Superintendent of Education, Re: Brandon Indian Residential School, 8 February 1957, LAC School Files Series, RG 10, Volume 7194, File 511/25-1-015.

48 Harry Atkinson [temporary principal at Brandon Residential School] to Rev. G. McMillan, United Church of Canada, Re—Our conversation over the phone—April 15th, 17 April 1957. United Church of Canada Archives MNWO/ANCC, Winnipeg, MB.

49 A.G. Leslie, Assistant Regional Supervisor, Department of Citizenship and Immigration, to R.D. Ragan, Regional Supervisor, 24 February 1958, RG 10, LAC School Files Series, Vol. 10358, File 511/6-1-015.

50 A.G. Leslie, Assistant Regional Supervisor, Department of Citizenship and Immigration, to R.D. Ragan, Regional Supervisor, 24 February 1958, RG 10, LAC School Files Series, Vol. 10358, File 511/6-1-015.

51 Te Hiwi, "Physical Culture as Citizenship Education," 145.

52 G. Swartman, Re: Voucher No. 206 dated March 10th/53—Poroo Taxi, Sioux Lookout.—$12.80, 23 March 1953, LAC, RG 10, c-13764, Volume 8274, File 494/6-1-014, Part 2.

53 Te Hiwi, "Physical Culture as Citizenship Education," 142.

54 Te Hiwi, "Physical Culture as Citizenship Education," 151.

55 Te Hiwi, "Physical Culture as Citizenship Education," 148.

56 "Remembering the Bad Old Days in the Residential School," 1972. Archived episode of CBC radio program *Our Native Land*, hosted by Johnny Yesno [former Black Hawk]. Available at https://www.cbc.ca/player/play/1402943356.

57 Te Hiwi and Forsyth, "'A Rink at This School.'"

58 Catherine Sherwood, Gary Osmond, and Murray G. Phillips, "Aboriginality, Racial Discourse and Football Media in 20th-Century Queensland," *Journal of Australian Studies* 44, no. 1 (2 January 2020): 101, https://doi.org/10.1080/14443058.2019.1668821.

59 Sherwood, Osmond, and Phillips, "Aboriginality, Racial Discourse, and Football Media," 110.

60 Richard S. Gruneau and David Whitson, *Hockey Night in Canada: Sport, Identities, and Cultural Politics*, Culture and Communication in Canada Series (Toronto: Garamond Press, 1993); Andrew Holman, "A Flag of Tendons: Hockey and Canadian History," in *Hockey: Challenging Canada's Game—Au-delà du sport national*, ed. Jenny Ellison and Jennifer Anderson (Ottawa: University of Ottawa Press, 2018), 25–44, https://doi.org/10.2307/j.ctt22rbkfw; Sam McKegney and Trevor J. Phillips, "Decolonizing the Hockey Novel: Ambivalence and Apotheosis in Richard Wagamese's *Indian Horse*," in *Writing the Body in Motion: A Critical Anthology on Canadian Sport Literature*, ed. Jamie Dopp and Angie Abdou, 1st ed. (Edmonton: Athabasca University Press, 2018), 167–84.

61 John Chi-Kit Wong, "Proem," in *Coast to Coast: Hockey in Canada to the Second World War*, ed. John Chi-Kit Wong (Buffalo: University of Toronto Press, 2009), viii.

62 McKegney and Phillips, "Decolonizing the Hockey Novel," 174.

Chapter 6: A Means of Escape

1 John "Jack" McDonald lived in Sioux Lookout after retiring from the NHL and played for the local branch of the Royal Canadian Legion.

2 Gary Osmond and Murray G. Phillips, "Indigenous Women's Sporting Experiences: Agency, Resistance and Nostalgia," *Australian Journal of Politics and History* 64, no. 4 (2018): 561–75, https://doi.org/10.1111/ajph.12516, 572.

3 Incidentally, as Alexandra and Kelly were discussing revisions to this section in early 2024, Kelly was halfway through reading the memoir of the widely admired Ojibwe hockey player Ted Nolan, who played for the NHL's Detroit Red Wings. Kelly saw some of his own experiences with racism mirrored in Nolan's life on and off the ice. Ted Nolan with Meg Masters, *Life in Two Worlds: A Coach's Journey from the Reserve to the NHL and Back Again* (Toronto: Viking, 2023).

4 Eric D. Anderson, "Using the Master's Tools: Resisting Colonization Through Colonial Sports," *The International Journal of the History of Sport* 23, no. 2 (2006): 247–66; Murray G. Phillips and Gary Osmond, "Marching for Assimilation: Indigenous Identity, Sport, and Politics," *Australian Journal of Politics and History* 64, no. 4 (2018): 544–60, https://doi.org/10.1111/ajph.12520; Janice Forsyth, *Reclaiming Tom Longboat: Indigenous Self-Determination in Canadian Sport* (Regina: University of Regina Press, 2020).

5 Chelsea Bond, Murray G. Phillips, and Gary Osmond, "Crossing Lines: Sport History, Transformative Narratives, and Aboriginal Australia," *The International Journal of the History of Sport* 32, no. 13 (2015): 1531–45, https://doi.org/10.1080/09523367.2015.1038704.

6 Bond, Phillips, and Osmond, "Crossing Lines," 1535.

Chapter 7: Visual Repatriation

1 Ann Fienup-Riordan, *The Living Tradition of Yup'ik Masks: Agayuliyararput; Our Way of Making Prayer*, 1st ed. (Seattle: University of Washington Press, 1996).

2 Kristen Dobbin, "'Exposing Yourself a Second Time': Visual Repatriation in Scandinavian Sápmi," *Visual Communication Quarterly* 20, no. 3 (2013): 128–43, https://doi.org/10.1080/15551393.2013.820585.

3 Naomi Angel and Pauline Wakeham, "Witnessing *In Camera*: Photographic Reflections on Truth and Reconciliation," in *Arts of Engagement: Taking Aesthetic Action in and Beyond the Truth and Reconciliation Commission of Canada*, ed. Dylan Robinson and Keavy Martin (Waterloo: Wilfrid Laurier University Press, 2016), 120, https://doi.org/10.51644/9781771121705-006.

4 Angel and Wakeham, "Witnessing *In Camera*."

5 Angel and Wakeham, "Witnessing *In Camera*," 123.

6 Celeste Pedri-Spade, "Waasaabikizo: Our Pictures Are Good Medicine," *Decolonization: Indigeneity, Education and Society* 5, no. 1 (2016): 45–70.

7 Paul Seesequasis, "Indigenous Archival Photo Project," https://paulseesequasis.com/.

8 Carol Payne, "Lessons with Leah: Re-reading the Photographic Archive of Nation in the National Film Board of Canada's Still Photography Division," *Visual Studies* 21, no. 1 (2006): 4–22, https://doi.org/10.1080/14725860600613147.

9 Carol Payne, "'You Hear It in Their Voice': Photographs and Cultural Consolidation among Inuit Youths and Elders," in *Oral History and Photography*, ed. Alexander Freund and Alistair Thomson, 1st ed., 97–114 (New York: Palgrave MacMillan, 2011).

10 Chelsea Bond, Murray G. Phillips, and Gary Osmond, "Crossing Lines: Sport History, Transformative Narratives, and Aboriginal Australia," *The International Journal of the History of Sport* 32, no. 13 (2015): 1539, https://doi.org/10.1080/09523367.2015.1038704; Michael Jackson, *The Politics of Storytelling: Violence, Transgression, and Intersubjectivity* (Copenhagen: Museum Tusculanum Press, 2002).

11 Payne, "Lessons with Leah," 17; Susannah Radstone, "Working with Memory: An Introduction," in *Memory and Methodology*, ed. Susannah Radstone, 1st ed (Oxford: Berg Publishers, 2000).

12 Annette Kuhn, "A Journey Through Memory," in *Memory and Methodology*, ed. Susannah Radstone, 1st ed. (Oxford: Berg Publishers, 2000), 183.

13 Linda Tuhiwai Smith, *Decolonizing Methodologies: Research and Indigenous Peoples* (London: Zed Books, 1999), 30.

14 Jane Lydon, "Return: The Photographic Archive and Technologies of Indigenous Memory," *Photographies* 3, no. 2 (2010): 179, https://doi.org/10.1080/17540763.2010.499610.

15 Heidi Bohaker and Franca Iacovetta, "Making Aboriginal People 'Immigrants Too': A Comparison of Citizenship Programs for Newcomers and Indigenous Peoples

in Postwar Canada, 1940s–1960s," *Canadian Historical Review* 90, no. 3 (2009): 427–62, https://doi.org/10.3138/chr.90.3.427.

16 The mural in the photograph is by C.W. Jeffries, and is titled "Indian Paying Homage to the Spirit of Chaudiere," https://www.cwjefferys.ca/indians-paying-homage-to-spirit-of-the-chaudiere. See "Remarks" about the paintings: "The 'Petun' (tobacco) sacrifice at the Chaudière Falls. The two paintings in this collection (1973-16-1 and 1973-16-2) were murals in the Chateau Laurier in Ottawa, part of a series of four images depicting important events in the history of the Ottawa River." See also Publication References, Marylin McKay, "Canadian Historical Murals 1895–1939: Material Progress, Morality and the 'Disappearance' of Native People," *Journal of Canadian Art History* 15 no. 1 (1992): 71, for further insight on this mural.

17 Jane Lydon, "'Behold the Tears': Photography as Colonial Witness," *History of Photography* 34, no. 3 (2010): 235–50.

18 "Indian Float Wins: All Fort William out for Giant Procession," *Daily Times-Journal*, 3 July 1951.

19 Eric D. Anderson, "Using the Master's Tools: Resisting Colonization Through Colonial Sports," *The International Journal of the History of Sport* 23, no. 2 (2006): 247–66.

20 Payne, "'You Hear It in Their Voice,'" 103.

21 Lynda Mannik, "Remembering, Forgetting, and Feeling with Photographs," in *Oral History and Photography*, ed. Alexander Freund and Alistair Thomson, 1st ed. (New York: Palgrave Macmillan, 2011).

22 Mannik, "Remembering, Forgetting, and Feeling," 86.

23 Mannik, "Remembering, Forgetting, and Feeling," 86.

24 Veli-Pekka Lehtola, "Our Histories in the Photographs of the Others: Sámi Approaches to Visual Materials in Archives," *Journal of Aesthetics and Culture* 10, no. 4 (2018): 8, https://doi.org/10.1080/20004214.2018.1510647.

25 Carol Payne, "Inuit, the Crown, and Racialized Visuality: Photographs from the 1956 Canadian Governor General's Arctic Tour," *Photography and Culture* 15, no. 4 (2022): 353–75.

26 Payne, "'You Hear It in Their Voice,'" 101.

27 Murray G. Phillips and Gary Osmond, "Marching for Assimilation: Indigenous Identity, Sport, and Politics," *Australian Journal of Politics and History* 64, no. 4 (2018): 559, 560, https://doi.org/10.1111/ajph.12520.

28 Benjamin R. Smith, "Images, Selves, and the Visual Record: Photography and Ethnographic Complexity in Central Cape York Peninsula," *Social Analysis* 47, no. 3 (2003): 11, https://doi.org/10.3167/015597703782352916.

29 Smith, "Images, Selves, and the Visual Record," 15.

30 Elizabeth Edwards, *Raw Histories: Photographs, Anthropology and Museums* (Oxford and New York: Berg, 2001), 19.

Epilogue

1 Fred Sasakamoose, *Call Me Indian: From the Trauma of Residential School to Becoming the NHL's First Treaty Indigenous Player* (Toronto: Penguin Random House Viking Canada, 2021); Survivors of the Assiniboia Indian Residential School and edited by Andrew Woolford, *Did You See Us? Reunion, Remembrance, and Reclamation at an Urban Indian Residential School* (Winnipeg: University of Manitoba Press, 2021).

2 TRC, *Canada's Residential Schools: The History, Part 2, 1939 to 2000* (Montreal and Kingston: Truth and Reconciliation Commission of Canada, 2015), 111.

3 We asked Annie's permission to use a detail of the necklace she gifted me on the back cover of *Beyond the Rink.*

SELECTED BIBLIOGRAPHY

Adams, Carly, and Jason Laurendeau. "'Here They Come! Look Them over!': Youth, Citizenship, and the Emergence of Minor Hockey in Canada." In *Hockey: Challenging Canada's Game—Au-Delà Du Sport National*, edited by Jenny Ellison and Jennifer Anderson, 111–24. Ottawa: University of Ottawa Press, 2018.

Anderson, Eric D. "Using the Master's Tools: Resisting Colonization Through Colonial Sports." *The International Journal of the History of Sport* 23, no. 2 (2006): 247–66.

Andrew, Brook, and Jessica Neath. "Encounters with Legacy Images: Decolonising and Re-Imagining Photographic Evidence from the Colonial Archive." *History of Photography* 42, no. 3 (2018): 217–38. https://doi.org/10.1080/03087298.2018.1440933.

Angel, Naomi, and Pauline Wakeham. "Witnessing *In Camera*: Photographic Reflections on Truth and Reconciliation." In *Arts of Engagement: Taking Aesthetic Action in and Beyond the Truth and Reconciliation Commission of Canada*, edited by Dylan Robinson and Keavy Martin, 93–134. Waterloo: Wilfrid Laurier University Press, 2016.

Armitage, Andrew. *Comparing the Policy of Aboriginal Assimilation: Australia, Canada, and New Zealand*. Vancouver: UBC Press, 1998.

Ba'abbad, Fatima. "History of Sioux Lookout Black Hawks Hockey Team, 1949–1951." Master's thesis, University of Western Ontario, 2017.

Bale, John. "Capturing 'The African' Body? Visual Images and 'Imaginative Sports.'" *Journal of Sport History* 25, no. 2 (1998): 119–37.

Ball, Jessica, and Pauline Janyst. "Enacting Research Ethics in Partnerships with Indigenous Communities in Canada: 'Do It in a Good Way.'" *Journal of Empirical Research on Human Research Ethics* 3, no. 2 (2008). https://doi.org/10.1525/jer.2008.3.2.33.

Banks, Marcus, and Richard Vokes. "Introduction: Anthropology, Photography and the Archive." *History and Anthropology* 21, no. 4 (2010): 337–49. https://doi.org/10.1080/02757206.2010.522375.

Barker, Adam J., Toby Rollo, and Emma Battell Lowman. "Settler Colonialism and the Consolidation of Canada in the Twentieth Century." In *The Routledge Handbook of the History of Settler Colonialism*, edited by Edward Cavanagh and Lorenzo Veracini, 153–68. Abingdon: Routledge, 2017.

Barman, Jean. "Sports and the Development of Character." In *Sports in Canada*, edited by Morris Mott. Mississauga, ON: Copp Clark Pitman, 1989.

Bloom, John. "The Imperial Gridiron: Dealing with the Legacy of Carlisle Indian School Sports." In *Carlisle Indian Industrial School: Indigenous Histories, Memories, and Reclamations*, edited by Jacqueline Fear-Segal and Susan D. Rose, 124–38. Lincoln: University of Nebraska Press, 2016.

———. "'There Is Madness in the Air': The 1926 Haskell Homecoming and Popular Representations of Sports in Federal Indian Boarding Schools." In *Dressing in Feathers: The Construction of the Indian in American Popular Culture*, edited by S.E. Bird, 97–110. Boulder: Routledge, 1996.

Bohaker, Heidi, and Franca Iacovetta. "Making Aboriginal People 'Immigrants Too': A Comparison of Citizenship Programs for Newcomers and Indigenous Peoples in Postwar Canada, 1940s–1960s." *Canadian Historical Review* 90, no. 3 (2009): 427–62. https://doi.org/10.3138/chr.90.3.427.

Bond, Chelsea, Murray G. Phillips, and Gary Osmond. "Crossing Lines: Sport History, Transformative Narratives, and Aboriginal Australia." *International Journal of the History of Sport* 32, no. 13 (2 September 2015): 1531–45. https://doi.org/10.1080/09523367.2015.1038704.

Brady, Miranda J., and Emily Hiltz. "The Archaeology of an Image: The Persistent Persuasion of Thomas Moore Keesick's Residential School Photographs." *TOPIA: Canadian Journal of Cultural Studies* 37 (2017): 61–85. https://doi.org/10.3138/topia.37.61.

Brown, Alison K., Laura L. Peers, and Members of the Kainai Nation. *Pictures Bring Us Messages / Sinaakssiiksi Aohtsimaahpihkookiyaawa: Photographs and Histories from the Kainai Nation*. Toronto: University of Toronto Press, 2006.

Carleton, Sean. *Lessons in Legitimacy: Colonialism, Capitalism, and the Rise of State Schooling in British Columbia*. Vancouver: UBC Press, 2022.

Charles, Grant, and Mike DeGagné. "Student-to-Student Abuse in the Indian Residential Schools in Canada: Setting the Stage for Further Understanding." *Child and Youth Services* 34, no. 4 (2013): 343–59. https://doi.org/10.1080/0145935X.2013.859903.

Chief, Arthur Bear. *My Decade at Old Sun, My Lifetime of Hell*. Edmonton: AU Press, 2016.

Comacchio, Cynthia R. *The Dominion of Youth: Adolescence and the Making of a Modern Canada, 1920–1950*. Waterloo: Wilfrid Laurier University Press, 2006.

Corntassel, Jeff, T'lakwadzi, and Chaw-win-is. "Indigenous Storytelling, Truth-Telling, and Community Approaches to Reconciliation." *ESC: English Studies in Canada* 35, no. 1 (2009): 137–59. https://doi.org/10.1353/esc.0.0163.

Cox, Bruce Alden. "Historical Anthropology." In *A Different Drummer: Readings in Anthropology with a Canadian Perspective*, edited by Bruce Alden Cox, Jacques Chevalier, and Valda Blundell, 31–40. Montreal: McGill-Queen's University Press, 1987.

de Leeuw, Sarah. "'If Anything Is to Be Done with the Indian, We Must Catch Him Very Young': Colonial Constructions of Aboriginal Children and the Geographies of Indian Residential Schooling in British Columbia, Canada." *Children's Geographies* 7, no. 2 (2009): 123–40. https://doi.org/10.1080/14733280902798837.

Dobbin, Kristen. "'Exposing Yourself a Second Time': Visual Repatriation in Scandinavian Sápmi." *Visual Communication Quarterly* 20, no. 3 (2013): 128–43. https://doi.org/10.1080/15551393.2013.820585.

Edwards, Elizabeth. *Raw Histories: Photographs, Anthropology and Museums*. Oxford and New York: Berg, 2001.

Evans, K.S., A. Lindsay, and N.J. Sinclair. "'Forced to Work 'Too Hard': A Case Study of Forced Child Labour and Slavery in Manitoba's Indian Residential Schools." *At The Forks* 1, no. 1 (2023). https://ojs.lib.umanitoba.ca/index.php/forks/article/view/921/933.

Fienup-Riordan, Ann. *The Living Tradition of Yup'ik Masks: Agayuliyararput; Our Way of Making Prayer*. 1st ed. Seattle: University of Washington Press, 1996.

Firpo, Christina, and Margaret Jacobs. "Taking Children, Ruling Colonies: Child Removal and Colonial Subjugation in Australia, Canada, French Indochina, and the United States, 1870–1950s." *Journal of World History* 29, no. 4 (2018): 529–62. https://doi.org/10.1353/jwh.2018.0054.

Forsyth, Janice. "Bodies of Meaning: Sports and Games at Canadian Residential Schools." In *Aboriginal Peoples and Sport in Canada: Historical Foundations and Contemporary Issues*, edited by J. Forsyth and A.R. Giles, 15–34. Vancouver: UBC Press, 2013.

———. "The Indian Act and the (Re)Shaping of Canadian Aboriginal Sport Practices." *International Journal of Canadian Studies*, no. 35 (2007): 95–111. https://doi.org/10.7202/040765ar.

———. "The Power to Define: A History of the Tom Longboat Awards, 1951–2001." PhD dissertation, University of Western Ontario, 2005.

———. *Reclaiming Tom Longboat: Indigenous Self-Determination in Canadian Sport*. Regina: University of Regina Press, 2020.

Forsyth, Janice, and M. Heine. "'The Only Good Thing that Happened at School': Colonising Narratives of Sport in the Indian School Bulletin." *British Journal of Canadian Studies* 30, no. 2 (2018): 205–22.

Francis, Daniel. *The Imaginary Indian: The Image of the Indian in Canadian Culture*. Vancouver: Arsenal Pulp Press, 1992.

Giancarlo, Alexandra. "Indigenous Student Labour and Settler Colonialism at Brandon Residential School." *Canadian Geographies* 64, no. 3 (2020): 461–74. https://doi.org/10.1111/cag.12613.

Giancarlo, Alexandra, and Janice Forsyth. "Indigenous Visual History: Remembering "Us" in Indian Residential School Hockey Photographs." *Journal of the Canadian Historical Association* 34, no. 1 (2024): 75–104. https://doi.org/10.7202/1112548ar.

Giancarlo, Alexandra, Janice Forsyth, Braden Te Hiwi, and Taylor McKee. "Methodology and Indigenous Memory: Using Photographs to Anchor Critical Reflections on Indian Residential School Experiences." *Visual Studies* 36, no. 4–5 (2021): 406–20. https://doi.org/10.1080/1472586X.2021.1878929.

Greig, Christopher J. *Ontario Boys: Masculinity and the Idea of Boyhood in Postwar Ontario, 1945–1960.* Waterloo: Wilfrid Laurier University Press, 2014.

Grimshaw, Anna. *The Ethnographer's Eye: Ways of Seeing in Anthropology.* Cambridge: Cambridge University Press, 2001. https://doi.org/10.1017/CBO9780511817670.

Gruneau, Richard S., and David Whitson. *Hockey Night in Canada: Sport, Identities, and Cultural Politics.* Culture and Communication in Canada Series. Toronto: Garamond Press, 1993.

Haig-Brown, Celia, Garry Gottfriedson, Randy Fred, and the KIRS Survivors. *Tsqelmucwilc: The Kamloops Indian Residential School—Resistance and a Reckoning.* Vancouver: Arsenal Pulp Press, 2022.

Hatfield, Philip J. *Canada in the Frame: Copyright, Collections and the Image of Canada, 1895–1924.* London: UCL Press, 2018.

Hirsch, Marianne, and Leo Spitzer. *School Photos in Liquid Time: Reframing Difference.* Seattle: University of Washington Press, 2020.

Holman, Andrew. "A Flag of Tendons: Hockey and Canadian History." In *Hockey: Challenging Canada's Game—Au-delà du sport national*, edited by Jenny Ellison and Jennifer Anderson. Ottawa: University of Ottawa Press, 2018.

Knowles, Norman. "'By the Mouth of Many Messengers': Mission and Social Service in Canadian Anglicanism (1867–1945)." In *Seeds Scattered and Sown: Studies in the History of Canadian Anglicanism*, edited by N. Knowles. Toronto: ABC Publishing, 2008.

Kuhn, Annette. "A Journey Through Memory." In *Memory and Methodology*, edited by Susannah Radstone, 179–96. 1st ed. Oxford: Berg Publishers, 2000.

Lederach, John Paul. *The Moral Imagination: The Art and Soul of Building Peace.* New York: Oxford University Press, 2005.

Lehtola, Veli-Pekka. "Our Histories in the Photographs of the Others: Sámi Approaches to Visual Materials in Archives." *Journal of Aesthetics and Culture* 10, no. 4 (2018). https://doi.org/10.1080/20004214.2018.1510647.

Lien, Sigrid, and Hilde Nielssen. "Absence and Presence: The Work of Photographs in the Sámi Museum, RiddoDuottarMuseat-Sámiid Vuorká-Dávvirat (RDM-SVD) in Karasjok, Norway." *Photography and Culture* 5, no. 3 (2012): 295–310. https://doi.org/10.2752/175145212X13415789392965.

Lunney, Gar. "Interview by Charity Marple." 7 May 1996. Canadian Museum of Contemporary Photography, NFB SPD collection, National Gallery of Canada, 1996.

Lydon, Jane. "'Behold the Tears': Photography as Colonial Witness." *History of Photography* 34, no. 3 (2010): 234–50. https://doi.org/10.1080/03087291003765836.

———. "Return: The Photographic Archive and Technologies of Indigenous Memory." *Photographies* 3, no. 2 (2010): 173–87. https://doi.org/10.1080/17540763.2010.499610.

MacDonald, David Bruce. *The Sleeping Giant Awakens: Genocide, Indian Residential Schools, and the Challenge of Conciliation.* Toronto: University of Toronto Press, 2019.

Malmsheimer, Lonna M. "'Imitation White Man': Images of Transformation at the Carlisle Indian School." *Studies in Visual Communication* 11, no. 4 (1985): 54–75. https://doi.org/10.1111/j.2326-8492.1985.tb00135.x

Mannik, Lynda. "Remembering, Forgetting, and Feeling with Photographs." In *Oral History and Photography*, edited by Alexander Freund and Alistair Thomson, 77–95. 1st ed. New York: Palgrave Macmillan, 2011.

Margolis, Eric. "Looking at Discipline, Looking at Labour: Photographic Representations of Indian Boarding Schools." *Visual Studies* 19, no. 1 (2004): 72–96. https://doi.org/10.1080/1472586042000204861.

Margolis, Eric, and Jeremy Rowe. "Images of Assimilation: Photographs of Indian Schools in Arizona." *History of Education* 33, no. 2 (2004): 199–230. https://doi.org/10.1080/0046760032000151456.

Maxwell, Krista. "Settler-Humanitarianism: Healing the Indigenous Child-Victim." *Comparative Studies in Society and History* 59, no. 4 (2017). https://doi.org/10.1017/S0010417517000342.

McCallum, Mary Jane Logan. *Indigenous Women, Work, and History, 1940–1980.* Winnipeg: University of Manitoba Press, 2014.

———. *Nii Ndahlohke: Boys' and Girls' Work at Mount Elgin Industrial School, 1890–1915.* Altona, MB: FriesenPress, 2022.

McCracken, Krista. "Archival Photographs in Perspective: Indian Residential School Images of Health." *British Journal of Canadian Studies* 30, no. 2 (2017): 163–82.

McKee, Taylor, and Janice Forsyth. "Witnessing Painful Pasts: Understanding Images of Sports at Canadian Indian Residential Schools." *Journal of Sport History* 46, no. 2 (2019): 175–88.

McKegney, Sam, and Trevor J. Phillips. "Decolonizing the Hockey Novel: Ambivalence and Apotheosis in Richard Wagamese's *Indian Horse.*" In *Writing the Body in Motion: A Critical Anthology on Canadian Sport Literature*, edited by Jamie Dopp and Angie Abdou, 167–84. 1st ed. Edmonton: Athabasca University Press, 2018.

Medina, William. "Selling Indians at Sherman Institute, 1902–1922." PhD dissertation, University of California, Riverside, 2007.

Miller, J.R. *Shingwauk's Vision: A History of Native Residential Schools.* Toronto: University of Toronto Press, 1996.

Milloy, John Sheridan. *A National Crime: The Canadian Government and the Residential School System, 1879 to 1986.* Winnipeg: University of Manitoba Press, 2017.

Mitchell, Lee Clark. "The Photograph and the American Indian." In *The Photograph and the American Indian*, edited by Alfred L. Bush and Lee Clark Mitchell. Princeton, NJ: Princeton University Press, 1994.

Montez de Oca, Jeffrey, and José Prado. "Visualizing Humanitarian Colonialism: Photographs From the Thomas Indian School." *American Behavioral Scientist* 58, no. 1 (2014). https://doi.org/10.1177/0002764213495027.

Narraway, A. "Settler Colonial Power and Indigenous Survival: Hockey Programs at Three Indian Residential Schools in Northwestern Ontario and Manitoba, 1929–1969." PhD dissertation, Carleton University, 2018. https://curve.carleton.ca/82934a96-9215-4d2c-b04d-76c685c480f0.

O'Bonsawin, Christine. "The Assertion of Canada's Colonial Self in National and International Sport." In *Sport and Recreation in Canadian History*, edited by Carly Adams, 275–302. 1st ed. Champaign: Human Kinetics Publishers, 2020.

Osmond, Gary, and Murray G. Phillips. "Indigenous Women's Sporting Experiences: Agency, Resistance and Nostalgia." *Australian Journal of Politics and History* 64, no. 4 (2018): 561–75. https://doi.org/10.1111/ajph.12516.

Palmater, Pamela. "Genocide, Indian Policy, and Legislated Elimination of Indians in Canada." *Aboriginal Policy Studies* 3, no. 3 (2014). https://doi.org/10.5663/aps.v3i3.22225.

Payne, Carol. "A Land of Youth: Nationhood and the Image of the Child in the National Film Board of Canada's Still Photography Division." In *Depicting Canada's Children*, edited by Loren R. Lerner, 85–107. Waterloo: Wilfrid Laurier University Press, 2009.

———. "Lessons with Leah: Re-reading the Photographic Archive of Nation in the National Film Board of Canada's Still Photography Division." *Visual Studies* 21, no. 1 (2006): 4–22. https://doi.org/10.1080/14725860600613147.

———. *The Official Picture: The National Film Board of Canada's Still Photography Division and the Image of Canada, 1941–1971*. McGill-Queen's-Beaverbrook Canadian Foundation Studies in Art History. Montréal: McGill-Queen's University Press, 2013.

———. "Through a Canadian Lens: Discourses of Nationalism and Aboriginal Representation in Governmental Photographs." In *Visual Communication and Culture: Images in Action*, edited by Jonathan M. Finn. Don Mills, Ontario: Oxford University Press, 2012.

———. "'You Hear It in Their Voice': Photographs and Cultural Consolidation among Inuit Youths and Elders." In *Oral History and Photography*, edited by Alexander Freund and Alistair Thomson, 97–114. 1st ed. New York: Palgrave MacMillan, 2011.

Pedri-Spade, Celeste. "Waasaabikizo: Our Pictures Are Good Medicine." *Decolonization: Indigeneity, Education and Society* 5, no. 1 (2016): 45–70.

Peers, Laura, Alison K. Brown, and Elizabeth Edwards, "Talking Visual Histories: Introduction." In *Museums and Source Communities: A Routledge Reader*, edited by Laura Peers and Alison K. Brown, 83–99. 1st ed. London: Routledge, 2003.

Penrose, Jan. "When All the Cowboys Are Indians: The Nature of Race in All-Indian Rodeo." *Annals of the Association of American Geographers* 93, no. 3 (2003): 687–705. https://doi.org/10.1111/1467-8306.9303009.

Phillips, Murray G., and Gary Osmond. "Marching for Assimilation: Indigenous Identity, Sport, and Politics." *Australian Journal of Politics and History* 64, no. 4 (2018): 544–60. https://doi.org/10.1111/ajph.12520.

Radstone, Susannah. "Working with Memory: An Introduction." In *Memory and Methodology*, edited by Susannah Radstone, 1–22. 1st ed. Oxford: Berg Publishers, 2000.

Regan, Paulette. *Unsettling the Settler Within: Indian Residential Schools, Truth Telling, and Reconciliation in Canada*. Vancouver: UBC Press, 2010.

Sasakamoose, Fred. *Call Me Indian: From the Trauma of Residential School to Becoming the NHL's First Treaty Indigenous Player*. Toronto: Penguin Random House Viking Canada, 2021.

Scherer, Joanna Cohan. "You Can't Believe Your Eyes: Inaccuracies in Photographs of North American Indians." *Studies in Visual Communications* 2, no. 2 (1975): 67–79. https://doi.org/10.1525/var.1975.2.2.67.

Sherwood, Catherine, Gary Osmond, and Murray G. Phillips. "Aboriginality, Racial Discourse and Football Media in 20th-Century Queensland." *Journal of Australian Studies* 44, no. 1 (2 January 2020): 97–113. https://doi.org/10.1080/14443058.2019.1668821.

Smith, Benjamin R. "Images, Selves, and the Visual Record: Photography and Ethnographic Complexity in Central Cape York Peninsula." *Social Analysis* 47, no. 3 (2003): 8–26. https://doi.org/10.3167/015597703782352916.

Smith, Linda Tuhiwai. *Decolonizing Methodologies: Research and Indigenous Peoples*. London: Zed Books, 1999.

Stalmach, Adele. "Native Women and Work; Changing Representations in Photographs from the Collections of the National Film Board and of the Department of Indian Affairs and Northern Development." Master's thesis, Carleton University, 1995.

Strathman, Nicole. "Student Snapshots: An Alternative Approach to the Visual History of American Indian Boarding Schools." *Humanities* 4, no. 4 (2015): 726–47. https://doi.org/10.3390/h4040726.

Survivors of the Assiniboia Indian Residential School and edited by Andrew Woolford. *Did You See Us? Reunion, Remembrance, and Reclamation at an Urban Indian Residential School.* Winnipeg: University of Manitoba Press, 2021.

Te Hiwi, Braden. "'Unlike Their Playmates of Civilization, the Indian Children's Recreation Must Be Cultivated and Developed': The Administration of Physical Education at Pelican Lake Indian Residential School, 1926–1944." *Historical Studies in Education/Revue d'histoire de l'education* 29, no. 1 (2017): 99–118.

Te Hiwi, Braden Paora. "Physical Culture as Citizenship Education at Pelican Lake Indian Residential School, 1926–1970." PhD dissertation, University of Western Ontario, 2015.

Te Hiwi, Braden, and Janice Forsyth. "'A Rink at This School Is Almost as Essential as a Classroom': Hockey and Discipline at Pelican Lake Indian Residential School, 1945–1951." *Canadian Journal of History* 52, no. 1 (2017): 80–108.

Thomas, Robina Anne. "Honouring the Oral Traditions of My Ancestors through Storytelling—Qwul'sih'yah'maht." In *Research as Resistance: Critical, Indigenous and Anti-Oppressive Approaches*, edited by Leslie Brown and Susan Strega, 237–54. Toronto: Canadian Scholars' Press, 2005.

Truth and Reconciliation Commission of Canada (TRC). *Canada's Residential Schools: The History, Part 1, Origins to 1939.* Montreal and Kingston: Truth and Reconciliation Commission of Canada, 2015.

———. *Canada's Residential Schools: The History, Part 2, 1939 to 2000.* Montreal and Kingston: Truth and Reconciliation Commission of Canada, 2015.

———. *They Came for the Children: Canada, Aboriginal Peoples, and Residential Schools.* Winnipeg: Truth and Reconciliation Commission of Canada, 2012.

Von Heyking, Amy. *Creating Citizens: History and Identity in Alberta's Schools, 1905–1980.* Calgary: University of Calgary Press, 2006.

Wells, Robert P. *Wawahte: Indian Residential Schools.* Vancouver: FriesenPress, 2016.

White, Bruce M. *We Are at Home: Pictures of the Ojibwe People.* St. Paul: Minnesota Historical Society Press, 2007.

Wong, John Chi-Kit. "Proem." In *Coast to Coast: Hockey in Canada to the Second World War*, edited by John Chi-Kit Wong. Buffalo: University of Toronto Press, 2009.

INDEX

Page numbers in bold indicate illustrations.

A

abuse: physical, 2, 51, 65–**67**, 83–84; sexual, xix
Alberni Boarding School, 44
Alexander, Harold (Governor General), 81
American Indian boarding schools, 39–40, 42–43
Anglican Church: administration of residential schools, 63–64, 70; archives of, 14, 60, 105; assimilation goals of, 39, 42, 71, 80–81, 138; sports and, 54, 61, 62, 85–86. *See also* Canada, Government of; residential school system
Anishinaabe (Ojibwe) people, xx
Anisininew: as language (Anishininimowin, formerly Oji-Cree), 10; as cultural identity, 49
anthropology, 29–31, 123–24, 134
Arcand, Eugene, 51
Assiniboia Indian Residential School, 23–24
Assiniboia Indian Residential School Legacy Group, 60
assimilation: forms of, 2, 4, 20–21, 34, 36–**37**, 39, 40, 44–46, 48–49, 51, 74–**75**, 86–87, 114, **115**, 123, 128; resistance to, 101–2, 114, 118–19; runaways, 1, 83–85
Australian Indigenous peoples, 14, 23, 86–87, 98

B

Beardy, Agrippa (Black Hawk), **109**
Beardy, Lawrence (Black Hawk), **109**
Benidickson, W.M., 63–64
Birtle Residential School, 3
Black Hawks: assimilation policies and, 21, 49, 123, 128, 130–31; establishment of, 71–72; hockey skills of, 98, 100; impact of the tour on, 94, 114; later lives of, 108, 137–38; life at Pelican Lake, 55, 82–83; media coverage of, 5, 74, 80–81, 86; photographs of, **7, 77–78, 90, 95, 99, 112–13, 126–27, 129**; reputation of, 73–74, 77, 82, 85–86; resisting assimilation on the ice, 118–19; tour as nation-building program, 15–17, 74, 104; tour engagements, 76–77, 81–82, 98, 102, 108–9; visual repatriation and, 4, 9–10, 14, 22–23, 25–26, 104–5, 121–22, 138–39. *See also* hockey; Pelican Lake Residential School; residential school system; individual players
Brandon Fair, 37–38
Brandon Indian Residential School, 5, 8, 36, 43, 48, 60, 71, 83
British imperialism, 19, 27–28, 38–39, 86. *See also* colonialism
Bull, George, **124–25**
Bull, Greta, 11
Bull, Kelly (Black Hawk): background, 11, 67–68; Black Hawks tour experiences, 101, 102, 128; child labour at Pelican Lake, 54, 55–57; community development work of, 94, 96–97; later life, 139; life at Pelican Lake Residential School, 9, 60–61, 68; on Indigenous culture, 118–21; on kind individuals, 55, 82, 90; on residential school denialism, 17–18, 87–88; on residential school education, 2, 53; on runaways, 85; on settler colonialism, 19, 21, 26, 118; on survival mechanisms, 53–54; on the unmarked graves

in Kamloops, 1; photographs of, **95, 99, 107, 109, 112–13, 126–27, 132–33**; physical abuse at Pelican Lake, 65–66, 83–84; relationship with hockey, xvii, 89–90, 97–98, 100, 102; remembering the Black Hawks, xvi, 71, 91, 108, 122–23; residential school compensation assessment, xvii, 58, 116–17; visual repatriation efforts of, 23–24, 104, 129–31

C

Canada, Government of: assimilation policies of, 8, 20–21, 41, 45–47, 51, 74; child removal policies of, 20, 53; immigration policies of, 45–46; policies vs practices, 57, 65; postwar culture and, 41–42, 49–50, 110; promotion of European gender roles, 16–17, 40, 43–44, 49–50, 60–61; promotion of sports, 42, 87–88, 100, 114, 136–37; residential school compensation assessment, 58; residential school funding, 19, 54, 62, 64, 66; restrictions of Indigenous performance, 111; settler colonial narratives of, 25, 28, 34–35; visual repatriation efforts and, 106. *See also* colonialism; Euro-Canadian culture; National Film Board (NFB); residential school system

Canadian Citizenship Branch, 45–46

Carpenter, Albert (Black Hawk), **75–77, 109–10**, 122, **126–27, 130, 132–33**

Carpenter, George (Black Hawk), **99, 112–13, 126–27, 130, 132–33**

Carpenter, Lawrence (Black Hawk), **109**

Chateau Laurier, 81, 98–**99**, 102–**3, 112–13**

Chicago Black Hawks, 71

Chief, Arthur Bear, 3

Christianity, 18–19, 68, 116. *See also* Anglican Church; colonialism; residential school system

citizenship education, 2, 45–48, 81, 128. *See also* Canada, Government of; colonialism; residential school system

colonialism: anthropology and, 30–31; assimilation policies under, 19, 20–21, 36–37, 44–45, 74–75; child removal practices of, 20, 53; emphasis on "civilization," 16–17, 39–40, 43; Indigenous family structures under, 8, 117–18; naming practices of, 105, 122; origins of, 18–19; resistance to, 101–2, 114, 118–19; restricting Indigenous cultural performance, 37, 86–87, 111; role of photography in, 9–10, 27–28, 33–36, 39, 50, 123; role of sports in, 2–3, 85, 87, 100; visual repatriation and, 14, 25. *See also* Anglican Church; Canada, Government of; racism; residential school system

Conacher, Lionel, **75–76**, 80

Cook, Henry G., 64–65, 73–74, 84–85

Cromarty, Annie, 10, 138, 141

Cromarty, Chris (Black Hawk): background, 6, 10; child labour at Pelican Lake, 55–57, 121; daily life at Pelican Lake Residential School, 68; later life, 134–35, 139; on abuse at Pelican Lake, 84; on assimilation policies, 53, 118; on Indigenous culture, 138; on kind individuals, 82; on residential school education, 2; on runaways, 1; on school staff, 66; photographs of, **7, 67, 95, 109, 135**; relationship with hockey, 91, 94, 98, 100–102; residential school compensation assessment, 58; Truth and Reconciliation testimony, 24, 65; visual repatriation efforts of, 4, 18, 111, 114, 117–18, 122, 129

Curtis, Edward, 33–34

D

Daily Bulletin, The, 72

Department of Citizenship and Immigration, 45–46, 74. *See also* Canadian Citizenship Branch; Department of Indian Affairs (DIA)

Department of Health and Welfare, 44, 74

Department of Indian Affairs (DIA): Annual Report, 39; assimilation policies of, 2–3, 9, 22, 27–28, 44–45, 61, 80–81, 85–86; Black Hawks tour and, 71, 73, 105; merger with Canadian Citizenship Branch, 45; public perception and, 4, 38; residential school education, 57–58, 138; residential school funding, 62, 64, 66; residential school sports,

2, 42, 44, 47, 83. *See also* Canada, Government of; colonialism; Department of Citizenship and Immigration
discipline: Anglo-Saxon values and, 41–42; assimilation and, 114; forced labour and, 36; at Pelican Lake Residential School, 63, 66–68, 102; sports and, 45, 47, 82–83; 137; surveillance and, 34
Division, The (Still Photography Division), 13, 14–15, 27–28, 34–35, **115**, 138. *See also* Lunney, Gar; National Film Board (NFB)
Doctrine of Discovery, 18–19, 21. *See also* colonialism
Dominion Day parade, 111, **115**

E
Edwards, Elizabeth, 134
Eisenhardt, Jan, 46–48, 73, **110, 132–33,** 140–41
Elkhorn Indian Residential School, 44
Euro-Canadian culture: anthropology and, 29; concept of ownership and, 18–19; gender roles in, 16–17, 40, 43–44, 49–50, 60–61; myth of civilization and, 30; sports in, 16, 42–44, 87, 136–37. *See also* Anglican Church; Canada, Government of; colonialism

F
Family Allowance, 53
Faries, Esther, 65
Fort Albany First Nation, 11
Fort William Sanatorium, 6, 8
Frost, Leslie (Premier), 53, 81
Fuller, William, 16, 76

G
Garden River First Nation Reserve, 46–47
Geraldton, 73
Goodwin, Grenville W., 16
Grand Council Treaty #9. *See* Nishnawbe Aski Nation (NAN)
Grierson, John, 14–15

H
Haskell boarding school, 43
Hewitt, Foster, 134
High River Industrial School (also known as Dunbow or St. Joseph's), 43
hockey: as an escape, 91, 94, 100–102; as assimilation tool, 2–3, 5, 9, 42, 82–83, 85, 114, 128, 130–31; Canadian identity and, 16–17, 40, 49–50, 86–87, 136–37; infrastructure of, 70; minor teams, 71–72, 80; resistance through, 101–2, 118, 137–38. *See also* Black Hawks

I
Indian Act, 20–21, 36–37
Indian and Eskimo Residential Schools Commission, 42
"Indian Braves, Calgary, Alta." (190?), 31–**32**
Indian Residential Schools Settlement Agreement, 53, 116–17
Indian School Bulletin, 47, 72
"Indians at the Fair" (1901), 36, **37,** 38
Indigenous culture: assimilation policies and, 8, 47–48, 53, 55; beading as a vessel of, 138; identity and, 137–38; knowledge sharing, 2, 119–21; preservation of, 118–19; reclamation efforts, 13–14; restrictions on performance of, 20–21, 111; settler framing of, 20, 32–33, 39–40, 46, 109–10; sharing of names, 105–6, 122–23. *See also* Canada, Government of; colonialism; Indigenous Peoples; residential school system; visual repatriation
Indigenous Peoples: agency of, 22, 101–2, 146n10; assimilation policies and, 20–21, 44–46, 49, 86–87; land rights, 19, 35; othering of, 29–30, 33–35, 41, 153n24; photographs by outsiders, 30–32, 37–39, 51, 109–10; reserves and, 19, 22–23, 36–37, 45, 46–47, 97; residential school survivors, 117–18; role of sports for, 74, 94, 96–98; settler opinions of, 73; visual repatriation efforts and, 23, 25, 104–6, 122–23. *See also* Canada, Government of; colonialism; Indigenous culture; visual repatriation
Inuit, 106, 123

J
Jefferson, Robert, **99**
Jones, H.L., 77, 80

K
Kainai Nation, 14, 29, 31

Kakepetum, Walter (Black Hawk), 80, 86, **99, 109, 112–13, 126–27, 130, 132–33**
Kamloops Residential School, 1, 42
Keesick, Thomas Moore, 39
King, Peter, 47

L
labour 2, 9, 20, 36, 52–53, 54–58, 62, 70, 88, 97, 116, 121, 137
Lac Seul First Nation. *See* Obishikokaang
Lamb, W. Kaye, **126–27**
Lebret Indian Residential School, 42
Leveque, Elga, 11
Longchari, Aküm, 25–26
Lunaape, 24
Lunney, Gar, 4, 13, 15–16, 21–22, **75–79**, **99**, 105–**7**, **110**, **112–13**, **126–27**, **129–30**, **132–33**

M
Macdonald, John A., 20
Mandamin, Eddie (Black Hawk), 77–**79**, **126–27**, **130**, **132–33**
Manitoba Indigenous Tuberculosis History Project, 24
Maple Leaf Gardens, 101
Marshall, J. (Principal), 61
Martin, Paul Sr., **75**, 81, 128
McCully, Bruce, 16, 17, 74, 76
McDonald, Johnny, 16
McDonald, Wilfred "Bucko," **75–76**, 80
Missionary Society of the Church of England in Canada (MSCC), 62
Moore, Percy, 63, 8
Morley Residential School, 43
Motion, J.R. (Principal), 44
Mount Elgin Residential School, 24
Munsee Delaware, 24

N
Naessens, J.R. (Principal), 43–44
National Film Board (NFB), 4, 14–15, 21–22, 49, 105. *See also* Black Hawks; Canada, Government of; Division, The; photography
Nishnawbe Aski Nation (NAN), 10
Norris, Malcolm, 53
North American Indigenous Games, 11, 96

O
Obishikokaang (Lac Seul First Nation), 11
Ojibwe people, xx, 23, 66, 105, 118, 120–21
Ojibwemowin (the Ojibwe language), 2, 10, 11, 66, 71, 105, 118
Old Sun Residential School, 3
Ontario Aboriginal Sports Circle, 11
Ottawa Citizen, 80

P
Pelican Lake Residential School: abuse of Black Hawks players, 2, 65–66, 83–84; child labour in, 54–57, 62, 70, 97, 121; comparison to reformatories, 53; daily life at, 68, 88, 121; deaths and disappearances at, 65; education at, 57–59; financial issues, 9, 61–62, 131; health issues, 62–66; hockey at, 3, 5, 70, 73, 82–83; overcrowding in, 59–60; photographs of **67, 69, 92–93, 103, 117**; public perception of, 63–64; recreation by gender, 60–61, 73–74; staff of, 8, 16, 43–44, 55, 62, 66, 71, 76, 83–84; staffing issues, 61
Phelan, Philip, 64, 81
photography: anthropometry and, 30–31, 123, 134; as marketing, 36–38; as propaganda, 15, 27, 29–30, 34–36, 115–16; colonial narratives within, 21–22, 33–34, 38–40, 48–50, 85, 109–10, 114, 123, 128, 138; critical analysis of, 4–5, 9–10, 28, 32–33, 51, 130, 136–37; history of, 29, 31–32; visual repatriation and, 13–14, 25, 122, 138–39. *See also* Black Hawks; visual repatriation
photo elicitation, 13–14, 104–5, 108–9, 111
physical education, 42–44, 46–48, 51, 60–61, 73–74, 85
Portage la Prairie Residential School, 48
potlatch, 20, 46
Prince Arthur Hotel, 94–**95**
Project Naming, 106, 115–16, 123
public perception: Indigenous performance and, 37–38, 86–87; residential schools and, 3, 8–9, 16, 24, 27, 36, 40, 80–81, 138; sports and, 16, 41–43, 87, 136–37. *See also* Black Hawks; Canada, Government of; photography

Q
Qwul'sih'yah'maht (Robina Thomas), 25

R
racism: anthropology and, 29–31, 123, 134; classism and, 50, 55; in media

coverage, 39, 61, 77, 86, 101–2; punishment for excellence, 98, 100. *See also* Canada, Government of; colonialism; residential school system
Rafton-Canning, Arthur, 35
Regina Indian Industrial School, 39
reserves, 19, 22–23, 36–37, 45, 46–47, 97. *See also* Canada, Government of; colonialism; Indigenous Peoples
residential school system: administrative issues in, 52, 70; as settler colonial tool, 3, 19, 20–21; assimilation policies of, 48–49, 74, 118, 123; child labour in, 2, 54–**56**, 62, 70, 97; child removal practices and, 20, 53; conditions in, 52–54, 118–19, 121; core tenets of, 1–2; denialism of, 17–18, 87–88; education issues, 2, 58–59, 117–18; financial issues, 9, 61–62, 131; gender roles in, 43–44, 60–61, 73–74; half-day system in, 54, 59–60; long-term effects on survivors, 1–2, 25, 67, 116–17, 118; origins of, 18–19; physical abuse in, 2, 51, 65–67, 83–84; public perception of, 5, 8–9, 16, 24, 27, 36, 40, 80–81, 138; restriction of communication, 6, 8; role of Christianity in, 18–19, 68; role of photography in, 21–22, 39, 48–49, 50, 85, 109–10, 114, 128, 138; runaways from, 82–85; sports and recreation programs in, 41–42, 45, 47–48, 50–51, 83, 137; survivors engagement with archival materials, 105, 134; visual repatriation projects and, 23–24, 106–7. *See also* American Indian boarding schools; Anglican Church; Canada, Government of; colonialism; Indigenous culture; Indigenous Peoples; Pelican Lake Residential School; specific residential schools
restorying, 4, 10, 22–23, 25–26, 105, 107, 121–22, 138–39. *See also* visual repatriation
Richard, Maurice "Rocket," 82, **95**
Ross, Jerry (Black Hawk), **77–79, 112–13, 126–27, 130, 132–33**
Round Lake Indian School, 3
runaways, 82–85

S
Sami people, 122–23
Sapay, Annie, 142
Sault Ste. Marie, 46–47
Schade, Arthur, 16, 70–71, 76, 81, 82, **109**
Seesequasis, Paul, 106
Seymour, Pete, 71, 82, 90, 119
Sherman Institute, 43
Shingwauk Indian Residential School, 58–59, 100, **124–25**
Shingwauk Residential Schools Centre, 14, 123
Sioux Lookout, 65, 71, 73, **120**
Sioux Lookout Meno Ya Win Health Centre, 10
Spence, Henry (Black Hawk), **109, 126–27, 130, 132–33**
sports, xviii, xx, 2, 16, 39–40, 41–46, 47–51, 60, 74, 80, 87, 94, 100–101, 140–41. *See also* hockey; physical education
St. Laurent, Louis, 45
St. Mary's Indian Residential School, 71
St. Peter's Residential School, 61
Strang, Matthew (Black Hawk), 123, **126–27, 132–33**
Strapp, Oliver Bailey (Principal), 8
Stringer Hall Residential School, 105
Swartman, Gifford (Indian Agent): involvement with the Black Hawks, 16, 45, 70–71, 76; on child labour, 56, 59; on health issues at Pelican Lake, 63–64; on recreation, 62, 83; photograph of, **109**

T
terra nullius (land belonging to no one), 19
Thomas Indian School, 48–49
Thomas, Robina (Qwul'sih'yah'maht), 25
Tintinalli, Oreste, 82, **109**
Truth and Reconciliation Commission, 24, 53, 65
Turner, G.R., 63
Tutsis, 30

U
United States, 20, 39–40, 42–43

V
visual repatriation: decolonization and, 107, 122–23; emotional challenges of, 131, 134; photo elicitation process, 108–9, 111; process of, 9–10, 13–14, 104, 121; Project Naming

and, 106, 115–16, 123; restorying and, 4, 25, 29, 105

W

Wesley, Angus (Black Hawk), **109**
Wesley, Bradley, 58
Wesley, David (Black Hawk): background, 11; Black Hawks tour experiences, 98, 128; child labour at Pelican Lake, 62, 70; hockey career, 100; later life, 58, 139; on residential school education, 57–58; photographs of, **95, 101, 106, 109–110, 112–13, 126–27, 130, 132–33;** visual repatriation efforts of, 24–25, 108, 111, 116, 122, 131, 134
Wesley, Elise, 11, 108
Wesley, Ernest (Black Hawk), **75–77, 109, 112–13, 126–27, 132–33**
Wesley, Frank (Black Hawk), **78–79, 99, 109–10, 126–27, 130, 132–33**
Wesley, Ronald, 57, 59, 85
Wickenden (Principal), 71
Williams, Barney, 25
Willie (Pelican Lake employee), 55
Wilson, Scott (Principal), 16, 66, 76, 83–84, **99**

Y

Yesno, Johnny (Black Hawk), 57, 85, **99, 110, 112–13**, 122, **126–27, 130, 132–33**

Perceptions on Truth and Reconciliation Series

ISSN 2371-347X

The Perceptions on Truth and Reconciliation series aims to bridge the knowledge gap between Western and Indigenous approaches to addressing historical and ongoing injustices in settler colonial states, repairing harms, and mitigating conflict across all levels and sectors of society. The series publishes new knowledge about how divided societies can design and implement more robust reconciliation mechanisms and processes to enable the creation of just and peaceful co-existence among diverse peoples both in Canada and across the globe.

6 *Beyond the Rink: Behind the Images of Residential School Hockey*, by Alexandra Giancarlo, Janice Forsyth, and Braden Te Hiwi, with the 1951 Sioux Lookout Black Hawks

5 *Did You See Us? Reunion, Remembrance, and Reclamation at an Urban Indian Residential School*, by Survivors of the Assiniboia Indian Residential School and edited by Andrew Woolford

4 *Sharing the Land, Sharing a Future: The Legacy of the Royal Commission on Aboriginal Peoples*, edited by Katherine Graham and David Newhouse

3 *Decolonizing Discipline: Children, Corporal Punishment, Christian Theologies, and Reconciliation*, edited by Valerie E. Michaelson and Joan E. Durrant

2 *Pathways of Reconciliation: Indigenous and Settler Approaches to Implementing the TRC's Calls to Action*, edited by Aimée Craft and Paulette Regan

1 *A Knock on the Door: The Essential History of Residential Schools from the Truth and Reconciliation Commission of Canada*, Edited and Abridged, by the Truth and Reconciliation Commission of Canada, with a foreword by Phil Fontaine